Come into the Water

A Survivor's Story

MERLYN JANET MAGNER

Come into the Water

SOUTH DAKOTA

STATE HISTORICAL SOCIETY

PRESS Pierre

This publication is funded, in part, by the Deadwood Publications
Fund provided by the City of Deadwood and the Deadwood Historic
Preservation Commission.

Library of Congress Cataloging-in-Publication Data
Magner, Merlyn Janet.
Come into the water : a survivor's story / by Merlyn Janet Magner.
    p. cm.
ISBN 978-0-9845041-1-4
1. Rapid City (S.D.)—History—20th century—Anecdotes. 2. Floods—
South Dakota—Rapid City—History—Anecdotes. 3. Magner, Merlyn
Janet. 4. Disaster victims—South Dakota—Rapid City—Biography.
I. Title.
F659.R2M35 2011
978.3'93—dc22   2010053004

The paper in this book meets the guidelines for permanence
and durability of the committee on Production Guidelines for
Book Longevity of the Council on Library Resources.

Printed in the United States of America

Text and cover design by Rich Hendel

Cover photograph by Rhonda Buell Schier

Please visit our website at www.sdshspress.com

15 14 13 12 11   1 2 3 4 5

for my beloved family in spirit

"Without knowing what I am

and why I am here, life is impossible."

—Leo Tolstoy, *Anna Karenina*

Contents

Friday, June 9, 1972

Rapid City, South Dakota

At approximately 10:25 P.M., I drowned.

Heavy rain and flooding burst through and filled the
canyon walls surrounding my family home. My mother,
my father, and my brother would drown that night, too.
I was swept away and landed on a rooftop, the only
survivor.

This is my story.

Prologue

After 9-11, I know many were moved to visit ground zero, and I sort of understood why. When these events happen, they are so outside the scope of our understanding, they beg comprehension. Most of us strive to fathom what happened. It is significant, beyond our ability to understand, and critical to assess. It demands our attention. We must face, honor, respect, and pay homage to those lost, find a way to bring meaning to them, and ask why.

After the flood, I was numb, detached, walking through yet another dream on the other side of some cosmic event. I wasn't the only one who didn't know where to file this one. Nothing this cataclysmic had ever come across anyone's radar in my neighborhood until now. From the outside looking in, there is a sense of disbelief and wonder—like knowing a train has careened off the tracks pell-mell. All hell has broken loose, and you can't stop yourself from taking it in and peering at what lies in the wake of the destruction.

A dear friend of mine was a television news producer for years, and she would tell me how it felt to literally "rush" to the scene, to be on a story that involved surprise devastation, fires, human interest stories that could stoke and poke at the heart of human fragility in a way that was impossible to ignore. It wasn't about simply conveying facts. It ignited the senses, like it or not. It was chemical: adrenaline, a high octane rush. Maybe it was true; we needed to see it to believe it.

Real horror is one thing; to make it up and manufacture it for entertainment is another phenomenon. I've noticed how our culture feeds on the fear factor, horror films, emphasizing tumult in all its forms, and I have always found it particularly disturbing. I knew what real fear was. I know what it can do to a person over the long term. I carried it with me, a constant and unwanted companion. We had an intimate and complex relationship, fear and I. It's not something I ever consciously

3

chose, bought a ticket to ride for fun, or a place I wanted to hang out indefinitely, not ever, but it eventually took up residence in my body just the same and forced me to respect its seeming power over me and my actions. The way so many others sought it out, eagerly paid for it, albeit superficially, made me think people must need the cattle prod, the jolt it provided in some way to feel something—alive, unfiltered epinephrine. I didn't get intentionally choosing fear when there are so many other, more interesting and higher vibrations. Why not pure joy, authentic excitement, exaltation, revelation, expansion? Stevie Winwood wanted "higher love" and John Lennon kept asking for truth. That tripped my trigger, floated my boat, made me want more, but I couldn't quite make it out.

Maybe it was the mystic in me that always needed to delve deeper to ultimately get to something higher, or conversely, look to the heavens to grasp a deeper knowing. I didn't like or need the external stimulants. I was stirred up enough. I craved ease. Nothing took the edge off the place inside that propelled me. But my story is about a state of mind brought on by a super-sized stimulant that forced me into a room I didn't want to dwell in.

It is not fair to judge anyone else's motives here. I'm willing to consider that my death experience had tweaked something in me, as well, that changed the way I perceived everything around me. I was a seeker, searching for more light. The dark side invited me in, but I didn't like the way it waltzed. It didn't make me move naturally, spiritually if you will, only physically, it seemed. The steps made me falter again and again. We all balance and move with fear. I had danced slow and long with it. Yeah, it made me feel alive, but not in a good way. In trying to avoid it, perhaps it split me down the middle even further.

I do not pretend to know.

This book is just my ride, my observations during a time of great upheaval. My perceptions are uniquely my own, the conclusions, the deductions I've gathered along the way, were reached much, much later. Back then I was hanging out in the "now," a skill that came so effortlessly in my youth, forever humming, straining to capture my music, a bit of magic dust left between the two worlds that I wasn't even aware I was straddling. The payoff would be expensive, along with the forgetting, but I wasn't contemplating or deliberating on anything too weighty just yet. I was merely wandering about, feeding my own wanderlust, close to the edge of my experiences, looking, listening, feeling light as air.

They say it takes great love and courage to volunteer for the roles we don in each others' lives, to bring the mirror up to our own faces for each other to fulfill the various assignments and contracts we came with, all made with the decision to be born again. Now here's where I may lose some of you and that's alright. I am not trying to convince anyone of anything here. But I believe we meet one another that we might make better choices for better outcomes, the free will part, and to enhance rather than hinder each others' paths. We are all related, connected to one another throughout time, the family of man. I believe this. We are all cohesive players in the grand production of each others' lives—the good, the bad, and all the rest agreed upon with near deft precision just the way we planned. My fervent hope is that we gently awaken, breathe, and remember why we came. Damn, it's time.

This book is not about payback; hence, I must add a brief disclaimer with regards to the identities of the many people I have included within the text. Many names have remained intact, including all those of my family. Others will be immediately known and/or recognized on the page by the reader, by way of public record, while there are those that are quite simply inconsequential, so their names have been changed or simply do not matter. It was never my intention as I set out to piece together the events of this crucial period of my life to harm anyone or further inflict injury upon anyone in the retelling of my life's journey. Again, this is my story, with the events told as honestly as I can place them upon the pages before you. Everyone who was witness to the night of June 9, 1972, in particular and those who were the players on the stage of my life fell behind the unique lens of my personal perceptions, and mine only.

We are living in extraordinary times that challenge the best in us. I find myself returning again and again to American Indian wisdom. It resonates within my heart like a deep clear pool of pure and untainted knowing that we can learn from. They lived by carefully chosen words and gracefully within the great mysterious silence that spoke to them in a myriad of ways through the natural world, the elemental kingdom, and the beating of one's heart. If one listens, I believe such wisdom is quite simply truth unvarnished, beautiful, transformative, and ultimately powerful. It lives, is timeless. Chief Seattle once said: "All things are connected. Whatever befalls the earth befalls the children of the earth." And Chief Dan George said, "My friends, how desperately do we need to love and to be loved."

We are born when the "water breaks." The earth is sheathed in it. I offer the reader an invitation of sorts, to "come into the water," as my father once invited me. I just can't guarantee that the water is fine. I can only promise you a ride, and aren't we all on a journey of our own design? This one just happens to be mine.

1955 or 1956
YMCA swimming pool, Flint, Michigan

My father is standing waist deep in the water near the edge with his arms outstretched, beckoning for me to come into the pool.

"Mernie . . . Come to me sweetie. The water's warm. I'll hold you."

I'm pint-sized, what would amount to a small sack of groceries in my father's strong embrace. I'm standing on the wet lip of the pool in my little flounced swimsuit, frozen, glued to the spot.

"Your daddy's here. I won't drop you darling. I promise I won't let anything happen to you, you know that." He is smiling at me, gently encouraging me. My brothers are nearby splashing about, happy.

I am becoming more and more frightened. I'm having trouble breathing. Now my face is flushed and I'm terrified. My mother is crouched behind me, waiting for this innocent moment of bonding to culminate in giggles and a child's joy. I don't budge.

I start to cry. My father continues to patiently coax me into his arms.

"Merlenska, what's the matter, dear heart? Nothing bad will happen. You're safe. *Come into the water*. I will hold onto you and I won't let go. Everything will be alright, you'll see."

Now I begin to choke and convulse. People stare. My tiny fists are clenched tight, my eyes sealed shut. I'm turning beet red. I want to scream, but nothing is coming out of my mouth. My mother leaps forward to throw a gigantic white towel around my shoulders and quickly picks me up.

Fade to black. . . .

1 The Pretender

Beverly Hills, California, February 2005

I was peeled back, exposed, raw, and vulnerable. I hurt inside and out. Newly returned from my second trip to Brazil within six months, I was planning to go back as soon as I could arrange it. Brazil was my last hope, my last resort. And this was no vacation.

I needed a miracle. I was running out of fuel. I was running out of time. I was running scared. Pain was a raging fire in my body. It scorched every breath I took. I was a wounded animal, my flesh gripped in an inhumane trap. I felt like road kill, like a wild animal now helpless, diminishing into the asphalt with the treads of tire after tire, each one of them another loss.

What had happened? How had I come to stand on this precipice, looking over the edge, wondering which was worse: a seeming illusion of solid ground beneath my feet or the free fall? When I became sick, it was as if God had thrown me a chair and ordered, "Sit down." I lived my life at warp speed. Maybe a head-on collision was inevitable.

I didn't know how surrender would feel. It was so easy for others to say, "Just let go." It sounded glib and trite to me. My life was on the line. I'd peered into the Pandora's box of my pain on countless levels in a never-ending pursuit of the truth behind it all. I'd spent my life seeking solutions and asking for understanding. I'd been on a dangerous recognizance mission only to return with no findings, no insight, nothing to show the world or myself who I'd become or where I'd gone. I'd exhausted the limitations of western medicine and every other kind of healing for that matter. It was a moot point. I turned towards heaven. There was only silence.

I am a chronic pain sufferer. I suffer from a trilogy of words that make people raise their eyebrows, a condition that makes them suspect a mental defect lies beneath pain that may or may not be real. But I am not unsound. I am a deeply flawed human being, but I have all my marbles. I am mentally strong and balanced. Box checked.

No, I am talking about physical, acute, bone-crunching, unrelenting, in-your-face, your-worst-nightmare, will-this-never-end, I'm-gonna-kick-your-ass pain. It has become my closest companion, my deepest confidant, the keeper of the lie.

I have lived a parallel life for seven years, with one foot firmly planted in this reality and the other just this side of hell. For over a decade I have lived on the edge of all reason, tested beyond the boundaries of my own endurance, flirting with death in an excruciatingly slow dance, always looking for a way to escape the misery of the step, a way off the floor and into what appeared to be a normal life.

And through it all, I've also been able to hear a hint of the sweetest music wafting through the ethers in the background . . . melodic, serene.

Around Thanksgiving in 1997, I was admitted to the emergency room with an irregular heartbeat, raging fever, and pounding headache. I hadn't been able to sleep for days because every time my head hit the pillow my heart fluttered a mile a minute.

A knowing friend asked if I was frightened. I was firm, emphatic. No. This was not a panic attack. It was physical. I was sick. My upper torso and head felt as if they were in a vice, as if all of my muscles had clamped themselves down hard around my nerve endings. My body suit felt like it didn't fit properly, like it was two sizes too small. I was off balance and hurt everywhere with pain that was as cruel as it was relentless.

After an exhaustive battery of tests, the verdict rolled in, a diagnosis, if you can call it that. I had an unnamed virus that enflamed my thyroid—my body's barometer—and in turn attacked my heart, which manifested in an irregular heartbeat. My whole body had kicked into overdrive. I perspired, feeling my heart pound, beating like a frightened sparrow, the organ stuck in overdrive, an unending high idle that kept me wide awake at night.

They put me on propranolol, a beta blocker, to regulate my heartbeat and told me to go home and rest. The doctor looked at me and said, "You're lucky it isn't Grave's disease." Whoa, sounded pretty grim.

My heart rhythm leveled out after many months of medication, but my head continued to pound. I was worried. Other than treating this disturbing and alarming symptom, this vague diagnosis was all the doctors could offer. The origin was unknown and would remain a mystery, along with the life I was dissecting. The 24/7 headaches never went away. As time went on, they became so severe that they took over my life. Since then I have been on a quest for answers and relief.

My quest took me down countless meandering roads. I sought out doctors of every degree, crisscrossing western and eastern traditions. I've done my time on the couch—you name it, I gave it my all, my best shot, overturned every proverbial stone. Freud, Jung, Reich. I spent infinite hours researching all medical modalities and then onto alternative medicines, exploring trauma and the way energy becomes trapped in the body. Early on there was no such thing as PTSD (Post Traumatic Stress Disorder). That came only after studying vets who began returning from Vietnam.

I knew about cellular memory, immobility response, and stress disorders. I practiced intense forms of yoga religiously for many years. I chanted, practiced breathing techniques, and meditated. I looked for and listened for God. He remained silent. I remained defiant.

I cleaned up my diet and my colon too. I practiced my prayer ritual. I studied all I could find on alchemy. Maybe I could somehow transmute this lead in my head to pure gold in my heart. I had psychic readings and past life regressions, boiled nasty brown herbs into cold dark tea, got stuck like a pincushion with the needles of numerous acupuncturists, and worked with my favorite chiropractor, all to no avail. It . . . I . . . was a huge question mark. My life and health were eroding, and I was helpless to stop it. The pain permeated every corner of my life, dogging me daily, pushing me, taunting me, and daunting me. It chipped away at my self-esteem, my fierce independence, and the easy confidence I'd always taken for granted. I was ashamed. I couldn't fix myself and neither could anyone else. I'd gone in with both barrels blazing. And here I was, firing rubber bands into thin air.

And on the other side of all this, I knew I possessed an innate, great capacity for joy, like the proverbial carrot that I could not reach. I searched and searched for the key. Chopra's *Quantum Healing*, Myss's *Anatomy of the Spirit*, Bradshaw's "wounded child." I read *The Bhagavad Gita*. I checked out where Buddha and the Dalai Lama weighed in on suffering and all the rest. I thought about karma, the mother lode of cause and effect. My apartment resembled a flea market, with piles of volumes stacked on the floor. No one I knew, including those I paid, had been here before.

All the while I pretended all was well. I avoided telling my friends about it, knowing that none of them wanted to hear me say, "I don't want to be in my body anymore. It's unimaginable." Pain can clear a room, silence the loudest person in no time flat. It makes others extremely uncomfortable, and who can blame them. No one wants to go there. It's a bore and a downer.

And this is where the lie begins. You are pretending now. Nobody wants to sit with it, spend time with it, least of all you. So you suck it up and move on, allowing everyone to remain comfortable, untouched and clean, off the hook.

The experts weigh in and scratch their collective heads. Friends throw up their hands. You're doomed, alone, weary, and looking for the white flag. Stranded in a land where no one speaks the language, and you can't read the signs. You're exhausted in a place that you don't know how to navigate out of.

Surrender . . . I didn't know what it looked like. So I kept on pretending.

2 Heartsick

My mother, Norma Elizabeth Anderson, was raised in Sturgis, a once quiet enclave in the southwestern corner of South Dakota. It has only become renowned of late because of the motorcycle races that are annually held there the first week in August. When my mother was growing up, it was simply a small hamlet on the fringes of the Black Hills, an outpost of larger Rapid City. The region was initially settled with the discovery and promise of gold.

Not one to let any grass grow under his feet, my great grandfather, H. O. Anderson, soon saw a business opportunity, not in the form of common prospecting and "striking it rich," but in commerce instead. He traveled to Yankton, on the opposite end of Dakota Territory, by wagon and proceeded to buy windows, doors, and all manner of building materials and began a millwork plant. He bought the existing J. G. Wenke Hardware Store and expanded numerous times. By 1890, the H. O. Anderson & Son Hardware was thriving, along with a furniture store, and by 1905 and 1907, he had added a tin shop and mortuary. His son, Earl H. Anderson, my grandfather and my mother's father, carried on the family businesses, expanded, bought a cattle ranch, and speculated in the stock market, where he made his own fortune.

My mother's upbringing was comfortable; however, I cannot say with certainty how life progressed for her growing up. I always sensed a "haunting" surrounding her demure demeanor, and only years later did I begin to put the pieces of the puzzle that was her childhood together. From the few pictures that remain, one adolescent photo stands out. She had huge dilated pools for eyes, a symmetrically perfect oval face, chiseled Roman nose, translucent skin, and thick, pouty lips. But her eyes reflect an unfathomable melancholy. When I hold this image, I feel like a voyeur staring into the bottom of her soul. It is sobering. She is too beautiful.

When I later married and moved to Seattle, this single black-and-white photograph disappeared in transport. It was my most precious possession, and I never quite got over losing it. I would come to learn over and over again in life that the most important things can indeed be carried in one's own arms.

My mother didn't care for her given name of Norma and preferred Elizabeth, her middle name, not Betty or Beth or Liz, but it never stuck. When she married my father, he called her simply NEM, for Norma Elizabeth Magner. She responded to my father's endearment from behind eyes of deep, abiding love. This affection rippled out, touching us all. She looked so delicate yet ardent. But she never spoke of her past. That was a foreign dialect that even she couldn't speak.

I never knew the depth of her anguish. I only detected it just beneath the surface, where it remained unexplored. She was an exquisite canvas, with no hint of the agony that went into its creation. No one spoke about their inner landscape in those days, much less shared it with their children. With regards to my mother, I simply didn't know then what I suspect now.

After spending her formative years in Sturgis, Norma went on to Saint Martin's Academy, a Catholic girl's school near Rapid City. She spent her final year of high school in Lincoln, Nebraska. The reason for this move mystifies me to this day, but I can take an educated guess. From there, she went on to pledge the Theta sorority at the University of South Dakota in Vermillion. I am not sure of her chosen major, but she eventually settled in Rapid City and began her career at KOTA, the local television station where her fate awaited her.

Dad graduated from the University of Minnesota and went off to serve in the Air Force during World War II. When he returned, he went to work as an anchorman for Channel 5 in Minneapolis. Later, opportunity knocked at Rapid City's KOTA, a smaller market, where I imagine him passing my mother in the dark corridor and their eyes meeting for the first time. Norma was a copywriter and worked in continuity. She possessed an effortless, elegant beauty that captivated my father immediately. He was dapper, her Cary Grant to his Veronica Lake. He loved her from the moment he laid eyes on her, but Mom was still carrying a torch for a soldier who came back from the war shell-shocked. He was never the same. For a time, she waited for him to really "come home," but he never did. The damage was done. He'd survived the battlefield, but he was gone.

Dad liked to tell the story of how he threatened to move to Australia and never return if she didn't make up her mind and marry him. Do they make them like that anymore? I ate it up with a spoon. My father didn't waste time.

Dad also ran sports commentary on the local news every night. Sometimes as a kid, I would go up to the television station with him for company, a special event because it was way after my bedtime. I was awestruck watching him carefully place tissue paper around his white shirt collar and powder his entire face to get camera-ready. It was oddly paradoxical to see him perform such a feminine act, for he exuded the ultimate masculine charisma.

He was untouchable, other worldly . . . that same indefinable quality I saw in my grandfather Ralph Magner and my mother. Dad smelled of Old Spice or Bay Rum, and I thought he walked on water. I used to sneak into the family room at 10:25 P.M. sharp to catch him on the late news broadcast. Having the TV on at the 10 o'clock hour was a Magner family ritual. We didn't see him much growing up, so stealing that glimpse of our dad on TV was cherished. When he wasn't at the studio, he was hitting the streets selling television and radio advertising. He sold "time," they called it. How ironic as there was so little left.

He held dominion over our family, at the helm of the Magner ship, rock solid and steady. He commanded respect and our valued trust. We gladly gave it to him. His life's purpose was making sure we had the best of everything to the best of his ability. We won the lottery with our parents, but we had no idea how blessed we were at the time.

When my mother married my father after meeting him there in the newsroom in Rapid City, they moved for a time to Flint, Michigan, where my father found other work. My two older brothers, Bill and Jeff, and I were born there in succession, and a family was made.

I came into the world last, behind them all. I was tiny and born with a heart murmur, but the long waited-for and wanted daughter just the same. I think my mother and I looked into each other's eyes knowingly, mutually and silently agreed, "It's good to see you again." We were old comrades.

Harry Truman was president. It was the year Albert Schweitzer won the Nobel Peace Prize, Anne Frank's *Diary of a Young Girl* was published in the United States, Dick Clark hosted the first American Bandstand, and MAD magazine was founded. It was 1952.

I grew up a half-pint and scrawny but filled with enough brawn to fight off bronchial pneumonia after I came out of the womb, with double-belted-steel resolve and enough energy to keep up with my older brothers most of the time. They were my personal guardians, and I came to count on their protection, along with the merciless teasing I endured. Fair enough.

Flint was a foreign country to me. I lived within the safe confines of my immediate neighborhood, where I played in the middle of the street with the boys until we had to move out of the way for the odd car to pass. I would walk over to my best-friend Nora's house and, instead of ringing the doorbell or knocking, stand in front, calling her name to come out and play in the abundant lilac hedges and rhubarb patches, to roller skate or, chalk in hand, hopscotch down the sidewalk.

Just before sundown on Saturday nights in the summer, we skipped to the end of the street, gathering friends along the way like flowers, to attend the outdoor free movies. Blankets and pillows tucked under our arms to tuck us under the stars on the slope of the deserted lot behind the old Shell gas station, where we watched Hopalong Cassidy and the Lone Ranger with his sidekick Tonto save the day.

The absolute best time was when we piled into Dad's Ford station wagon for a trip to the drive-in movies. We'd make that same bed of comfort in the back with the seats turned down, squirming around, inducing mayhem, throwing popcorn at each other, and finally falling fast asleep in the middle of *The Ten*

Commandments, way before Moses got the chosen ones across that Red Sea.

I always wondered if that sea really was red and why? Always wondering . . . were we chosen, not chosen? Why? And what about all those Acts of God, miracles? It was big stuff for a kid with a wild imagination and a belief that anything was possible. I wanted more. I always wanted more—more life, more answers, more magic. Could one simply command it and make it so? Could I?

Of course, there was the building of a fort in the backyard with old sheets and our own secret codes, staving off sleep by swapping ghost stories with the boogie man in attendance or the ever present man in the moon. The primary goal was to be under the endless canopy of night sky, looking up. My brothers nicknamed me Moon Baby, or Moon. My father called me Merlenska, or Lenska for short, sometimes Moulon. Go figure.

Dad and I liked big dogs, and over the years we had a menagerie of Great Danes, German shepherds, boxers, but inevitably Mom would end up taking care of them, so they shrank over the years until, at the end, there were only two nervous miniature poodles.

We rode our bikes like bandits down steep, cracked, and gravel roads. I had a need for speed even then, and life was fine until I hit a rock and careened over the handlebars one day, escaping serious injury as I was wont to do. This episode produced my second head wound and first black eye. My mom's father had dropped me on a brick floor when I was an infant. My head must have been made of iron ore to go along with all the other metal inside. I just defied my body.

By the time I turned seven, we had packed the family into the dusty sky-blue Ford station wagon with the wood panels, along with our cat Cleo and George our dachshund, and moved back to South Dakota. Dad felt that Flint was expanding too quickly and the neighborhood along with it. I think my mother probably filled his head with visions of small-town life in the safer environs where she had grown up and convinced Dad that we ought to get out while the getting was good. And after all, they had met in South Dakota, and Dad liked the idea of being a big fish in a smaller pond, I think, but this idea is mere conjecture on my part. I am sure there were many conversations behind closed doors making plans for our future. But once the issue was decided, Dad was welcomed back into television broadcasting in the familiar fold of mid-America where a growing family could thrive and flourish. We lived in Sturgis for a time with my mother's parents, and Dad commuted to work at the TV station, until we could get on our own feet.

My grandmother Helen, "Mamba" to me, was a gentle woman. She could always be found in her kitchen. She taught me how to bake and gave me my first cookbook. I can see the pink rose-petal and green-leaf patterns embroidered on her cotton apron and smell the peanut-butter cookies and German chocolate cake coming out of her oven, while hot tapioca came to a boil on the stove.

Her home was spotless, the wood floors and dark mahogany furniture gleaming with polish and a hint of fresh lemons. She was quite immaculate, from the confines of her home to the precision with which she would ensconce herself in the first pew at Blessed Sacrament Church every Sunday with rosary beads in hand, a white lace doily on her head, silently mouthing prayers to the Virgin Mary. What were behind those whispered pleas inside her faith I wondered? From the look in her eyes, I knew she wasn't just reciting words.

And even though I also remember her emptying the thick glass ashtray that she managed to fill every night, I saw nothing out of the ordinary, nothing to suggest that a river of misery ran just beneath the façade of genteel perfection and permeated the lovely house she kept along with those clandestine worlds I knew nothing of.

My grandfather Earl, "Gopa" Anderson to me, was another story . . . an imposing brute of a man, tall—well over six feet—with thick short-cropped silver hair and clean starched shirts. He smelled like fresh soap and bubble gum, a brand of chewing tobacco he favored.

He was also a handful, a raging alcoholic. I never questioned why he would chase me around the living room letting his false teeth clack and fall onto his tongue with glee. I was terrified and with good reason. He could be a real scary human being, an unpredictable giant who might swallow me whole with a simple backward glance. When he cackled and wheezed with that glazed expression on his face, I would run in the opposite direction, screaming for my life.

He was a bear of a man with blank, bloodshot eyes. He drove a big beige Buick that seemed like a tank to me, a vehicle made more for warfare than mere traveling. I never felt safe around him, and I don't think my mother did either.

As I was growing up, the telephone often rang in the dead of night. Then my father would go to pick up his father-in-law from some nameless bar and deposit him back home before dawn to sleep it off. My mother, mortified, suffered in silence behind closed doors. I can only imagine the horror and torment he subjected her to when she was a defenseless child and he in a booze-drenched rage was entertaining his ever-present demons.

The air was dense with deception and disappointment. Why didn't Mom want him near us, I mused? Why did Mamba look so sad and Mom so mad? Family portraits usually resemble an innocuous Norman Rockwell painting from the outside; a balanced composition, careful brush strokes, and evenly distributed color. We all know that underneath the surface, there can often be a far more complex reality. Ours was no exception.

My mother's older sister, Mildred, was not around when I was growing up. She married Brigadier General Raymond Dunn in the Air Force, and he was posted overseas. The regular packages of socks and pajamas she would faithfully send early every Christmas always marked the beginning of the season, along with the unveiling of the Nativity scene.

I gleefully unwrapped the set and assembled it near the tree. I thoughtfully moved the figures around the manger ever so gently until baby Jesus was placed just so. Then I would stare into that serene infant's face, searching for the answer to something. The figures were meaningful to me, and I was especially spellbound by the Wise Men bearing gifts.

What knowledge did they possess that I didn't, I innocently wondered? And how did they find it in the stars? How did things line up so that they knew "the moment" of such a significant event had arrived and it was time to show up? I wanted to know more, but all that astronomy, astrology, and intrigue could wait. There was an enormous white-flocked tree to trim, other gifts to behold, and songs to be sung. When we raised our voices, it was in unison and praise.

A story about my Aunt Mildred bares the impact her life was to make upon my own. The year I turned sixteen, I got to visit my favorite cousin, Mildred's daughter Sug, in Germany. While there, we made a pilgrimage to Lourdes, France. For Catholics, this trip was akin to a trek to Mecca.

It was in Lourdes that Saint Bernadette, who had experienced unimaginable physical pain in her short life, witnessed visions of the Virgin Mary, who told her to dig in the ground until a natural spring came forth from which healing properties flowed. Bernadette herself never benefited from the spring. It would be her undeterred faith that sustained her. I'll never forget the Blessed Mother telling her, "I cannot promise you happiness in this life, only the next." I had to think about that. I had no formed beliefs surrounding my Roman Catholic upbringing. I was just a sponge. At around the age of five or six, I tried one night to get my brain around the idea of eternity; when I closed my eyes to find only darkness, it scared me silly, and I ran to my mother's bed. These thoughts were too big and I was humbled by them.

Lourdes was filled with vendors selling rosary beads, plastic bottles of Holy Water, and statuettes of the Virgin Mother. I had never seen so many wheelchairs, and most of the people who sat in them smiled, their faces reflecting the hope they held for healing their broken bodies. All those trinkets were just a front for the hope inside them. I felt the mystery of it, but I was certainly not among the sick and seeking. Instead, I reveled in the fact that I was sixteen, in the company of my gorgeous cousin, and in France. That was miracle enough for me.

Years later, after Mamba died and Gopa was grieving and drinking himself into an early grave, the local monsignor stepped in to play matchmaker and introduced my grandfather to a church worker who "cleaned his clock," and by that I mean his checkbook. That episode took the bloom off the rose between the church and my mother. The veneer on her faith was irreparably cracked, and the fate of our religious upbringing sealed. She promptly pulled my brothers out of parochial school, and I would never get to wear the dark-green and blue-plaid uniforms of Saint Martin's Academy, nor attend their brand-new school, with the brand-new dormitories in the hills that I coveted so.

My mother's love for us was fierce, and it was from her that I knew and felt complete, unconditional love. She left me this legacy, credentials greater than any diploma from a school I never attended. She indulged and spoiled me. When I didn't feel well, she would say, "Just sleep in this morning, little one." Even if I was pretending, she would bring me beef bullion, soda crackers, and 7UP on a tray and slip me broken pieces of white almond bark from Fanny Farmer.

I think she allowed this indulgence so that we could wile away the day together, bask in one another's presence. And delightful it was, snuggled up in the safe arms of family, out of harm's way. Nothing bad could ever happen in this lovely cocoon.

She was demonstrative, affectionate, tender, and magnetic. I would naturally gravitate to her wherever she was sitting and, like a cat, curl up at her feet, my head leaning into her smooth bare summer legs, my eyes closed, content, inwardly purring. My hair was always long, and often I would fetch my brush and entice her to gently run it through my hair while we talked. She never made me feel self-conscious, awkward, or unimportant. She told me how she had waited and prayed for me, a daughter. She called me her light.

Her warmth and maternal nature were so compelling that some of my friends even took to calling her Mom, which she considered a high compliment. She was wise, lovely, and, of course, flawed. At times she could be far away and aloof, contemplating her own histories and mysteries. She could just stop in mid-sentence and leave the room, disappear. She might not come out for hours. I knew she was rare. She was one of those "who walks in this world, but is not of it." Life was an obstacle course for her. Her furrowed brow and those haunting eyes told me this. Her heart was broken in too many places, which was not lost on me. Child that I was, I felt it all and wanted to hold her and protect her in the same way she held and protected me and all those lucky enough to enter her soft aura.

We were just kids when my best friend Deb and I attended a school dance across the street from my house. We dressed to the nines in our rick-rack-trimmed skirts and puffed sleeves, stepped off the curb in our "hood," and traipsed into the gym for what we thought would be the best experience of our lives.

Many years later, Deb, always painfully shy, told me that the dance was torture for her. She feigned sickness, and back across the street she trudged into our home, where she soaked up my mother's love and understanding. Mom drew her a warm comforting bath, erasing all rejection, soothing away the blues she also kept for company.

My mother often came up behind me, wrapped her arms around me, and asked, "Do you know how much I love you, darling?"

I took it for granted. I assumed everyone's parents loved them in this way. In my little kingdom, love was the order of the day, and I reigned supreme.

When I was twelve, something rocked my childlike world. My mother and father seemingly disappeared into thin air, and Jen, my paternal grandmother, flew in from cold Duluth, Minnesota, where Dad had grown up. She appeared like an apparition on our doorstep. It must have been winter because I can still feel the cold, smooth down of her full-length mink coat as we hugged.

She was a vision in her black hat with its black veil floating over her white powdered face and scarlet lips, the pungent smell of Estée Lauder's eau de parfum wafting behind her as she made her way into the room, slipping off her black high-heeled rubbers, with the top black buttons open. She was prepared to take over, loving but serious.

Mom and Dad were in Rochester, Minnesota, at the Mayo Clinic. Mom was sick, we were told, but everything would be alright. But it didn't feel alright. I reached into my protected memory and felt around. Hadn't Mom just had an operation at the local hospital not too long ago? Bill, Jeff, and I were so cushioned and shielded from reality. She'd simply been gone for awhile, her absence explained away well enough, and then she reappeared as if she'd been out to lunch. Mom had come back, subdued, but home. What else mattered? We had settled into life again without mention of illness or, God forbid, danger. Mom was among us again, albeit thinner, and life went back on course.

But now even I, small and cloistered twelve-year-old that I was, knew something was seriously wrong. It had to be something important to have drawn my mother away from her proper place, safe in the fold of her family. My mother had just had her second major heart attack.

When she arrived home again several weeks later and I was led into her bedroom, I was scared. The mother that I knew and loved wasn't there. In her place was a frail, pale, and tinier version. She softly whispered to me to come over to her and sit down. I was tentative and nervous, my mouth dry. I felt flushed. My heartbeat quickened, and my hands were clammy and damp.

She looked like she might break if I even moved or ventured over to her. When I did, she lightly caressed my wrist, pressed her thumb into my palm to make a point, and said, "I missed you so much." Oh, Mom. "Do you want to know what happened to me while I was gone?" I was taken aback. What could she possibly mean? I stiffened. I glanced up at my father standing next to the bed in their darkened bedroom, and he seemed doubtful too.

And then, in the softest whisper, barely audible, she said, "I don't want the children to be afraid of what they cannot see." And with that, she pulled up her nightgown and showed me the most extraordinary thing. From the tip of her collarbone, vertically, and all the way down her chest and past her belly button was a wound so deep and red and raw that it took my breath away. On either side were what looked like miniature metal suction cups evenly spaced, and from them, crisscrossed like shoelaces, thick black thread held my mother's body together.

I was stunned, speechless. What had they done to my mother? And why? Was she alright? What else was going to happen? I was dumbstruck, to put it mildly, and confused.

At this moment, I first sensed that there were no guarantees in life, and this thing we were all doing here was not permanent. The thought was too grave for a child my age. I thought it, felt its heavy weight, but could not grasp it. So, after planting an abbreviated child's kiss on her cheek, I went quickly and quietly from the room and into the sanctuary of my soft pink bedroom, where I opened up my latest Nancy Drew/Trixie Belden mystery. I began reading on exactly the same page I had left off, not missing a beat or a breath.

I used to believe that it was at this point when my chief coping skill—denial—first kicked in, but perhaps it was in place much sooner. Throughout my life, I would retreat into the world of books whenever and wherever I was; for escape, answers, comfort . . . or to simply turn the page . . . on another mystery. I never looked back.

3 A Beautiful Day

Rapid City, South Dakota, June 9, 1972

It was a beautiful day, perfect really, in the Black Hills, an island of mountains in the Great Plains of America. I slept in that morning, as was my guilty pleasure always. California was behind me, and here I lay in my old bedroom looking up, the ceiling papered in a riot of red peonies. I awoke without a care in the world and breathed deeply into the new day, grateful. Yes.

I was home.

I stretched, yawned, and thought about how I might toss a Frisbee around the park with old friends or curl up on the couch with my brother Jeff and catch up. He had just flown in the night before from Tempe, Arizona. But there was time. Everyone was in town, it seemed—the old band Jeff played in, my friends who were scattered across Colorado or from the University of South Dakota in Vermillion, and me. I was fresh off the coast in my powder-blue '66 Mustang convertible with the top down, my waist-length tresses tied up in a ponytail and Joni Mitchell on the eight-track singing "Chelsea Morning." Her lyrics described my life, a life in which, wow, the sun really did pour "in like butterscotch" and tickled all my senses.

The West Coast sunshine had tinted my caffè-latte skin, sprouting the few freckles I could still count across the bridge of my nose. I was nineteen. I felt so free. Fearless. I was alive, innocent, and expectant. The laid-back days of summer had arrived. Life was good.

Then it started to rain. No problem. Put the rag-top up, work the phones, and relax. It had been raining off and on for the better part of the week, but as this particular day began, there was only a slight breeze, not a rain cloud in sight, yet. Besides, a little rain wasn't going to put a damper on this summer of love. When the thunder clapped overhead, I would whoop with wonder. I always loved a good storm, especially if there was some noisy electricity to go along with it. The more dramatic the better.

The air was moist. It smelled so pure and new. It matched the way I was feeling, unformed and abstract, yet bursting with the possibility of what shape I might take. I sensed that something was going to happen, something important, but what? Whatever it was . . . I would be ready.

Our home was my dad's dream. It was a "House Beautiful" home located in a canyon, just steps away from a cold but tranquil creek. When we were kids, we ran its rapids on big black rubber inner tubes. On those long perfect summer days, I would paddle madly to keep up with my brothers—me the sole, tawny tadpole of a sister, the runt tagging along behind, always trying to catch up, eager to belong. I remember being scared, yet exhilarated more often than not, going for it, "piercing the envelope," and getting trapped in the current.

I would slam into a protruding boulder or get snagged by a large overhanging branch, my skinny bottom and long limbs flying over the side or slipping through the hole in the tube's center. More than once, I'd get caught and sucked down, disappearing, gulping for breath . . . knowing that my brothers would come to my rescue. Sure enough in the nick of time, they pulled me from the creek like a drowned cat, red-faced, coughing, and exclaiming how lucky we were that we didn't lose the all-important tube.

We survived many covert encounters with the mysterious forces of nature. Yeah. We were comfortably naïve, always confident, dismissive of danger. And mum was the word when it came to these perilous underwater escapades and close calls, so easily forgotten until the next time. Mom and Dad, as cool as they were, didn't need to know we just nearly drowned for the umpteenth time. After all, we were masters of our universe, reckless, magical children on the cusp of a brave new world, a wide-eyed revolution of youth. We could feel, touch, and taste it. You couldn't tell us anything. We knew what life was.

And so Jeff and I played that June day. I went to the little park off Mount Rushmore Road, Rapid City's main drag, and tossed a Frisbee around. I caught up with and chatted up some cronies I hadn't seen since I'd moved to Los Angeles the year before. In high school, before we graduated, we spent most weekends here. We'd cruise the boulevard in our cars, squinting into the night looking for mischief, new flames, or old friends. The music would be turned up full blast. They would know we were coming from a mile away. My friends and I were like romantic heroines at the helms of our cars. Like seasoned sailors, we were ready for adventure at a moment's notice. We were at the keel, in full command of our destinies . . . or so we thought.

This June day was like any other when it began, unspectacular. Its details were being stitched into the fabric of our lives, as ordinary as well-worn denim. It was just another day in our young lives, nothing to worry about, not a care. We weren't concerned with international events, or our own survival for that matter. Heck, we didn't even have plans for the evening.

Back home now after a lazy afternoon, it had begun to rain. I looked up at the sky to see clouds of unusual, marvelous shapes. I started humming along to the strains of Joni Mitchell's "Both Sides Now" and tried to imagine the folk singer's inspiration when she wrote the song. She, a painter of words, images, and feelings, was a Libra like me. I'd never heard lyrics like hers before. I knew them all by heart, but especially the strain that went, "So many things I would have done, but clouds got in my way. . . . It's life's illusions I recall, I really don't know life at all."

My parents were popular and social animals who complemented each other nicely. You could feel the love they shared. It was palpable and apparent to anyone in their presence. They enjoyed the cocktail hour as much as any established, life-loving couple in their early forties, and that evening was no different. They walked across the street to have a drink on our neighbors' patio, where they could listen to the creek and watch it rise.

Although our house was situated on a nice roomy plot of land on what is now Magic Canyon Road, outside the city limits and below the ascent into the hallowed hills, we did have neighbors. Next door, I babysat occasionally for the William Houghs and their newly adopted infant boy, as I did farther down the canyon for Dr. Crowder, a brain surgeon, who had a brood of beautiful sons. Across the street at the entrance to the cul-de-sac lived the Smith family, who would entertain my parents on the night of the flood and drown along side them. The only other house, a dark brown ranch-style dwelling, belonged to Mrs. Knecht, who lived alone, her back stoop bordering the creek bed. Her son Richard was the architect who had designed and built our home. I babysat their adorable red-headed son Jim in their A-frame home farther up in the Hills. Richard was handsome, charming, and hip in a Robert Redford kind of way. His wife, Ting, was lithe and graceful like a ballerina. Both were quiet, calm, artistic, and thoroughly enchanting.

Our house was a bit of a showcase at the time, one of Richard's first projects, and he had attacked it with carte blanche. There were plush, wild-striped, multi-colored carpets and tactile surfaces galore, from the golden grass-cloth walls to the Belgian crewelled-linen fabrics covering the furniture. Even the lighting was sophisticated and soft with ornate fixtures protruding from unexpected surfaces. When I said how much I loved my red wallpaper, he suggested we cover the ceiling, too, and I would feel like I was on the inside of a gigantic supernatural gift. Why not? There were no rules with Richard's creativity and talent. My mother insisted on Early American accents spaced throughout, but it all blended together into what was for the time an unusual and fun place for us to gather with our friends. The sound of laughter and music echoed through our halls and into those canyon walls regularly, until, inevitably, Mom would plead with us, "Please turn the stereo down."

I know she liked some of it, though, and once caught her singing along with Judy Collins, "And I think it's going to rain today."

There was one particularly auspicious summer night when, after an Electric Prunes concert had ended (and my parents were on their way to Las Vegas for some sun and gambling fun), I boldly invited the band to come over after the show. I'd never seen an array of so many people collected at one house, and the majority of them were strangers to me. It was a free for all, a real spectacle.

Only later did I find out that our folks never made it past the city limits that night. They had car trouble and ended up in the Holiday Inn on the outskirts of town. Had they come home instead, there would have been hell to pay. Looking back, I know it was dumb luck that some derelict druggie didn't make off with the family silver. We miraculously put our father's house in order without so much as a broken glass or a cigarette burn, but I never brought another concert home again. I was learning first-hand about close calls and bad-boy bands.

My brother Jeff and I hadn't had a chance to really catch up. This Friday night, we were grateful to have the house to ourselves and be able to talk freely about all of the adventures we'd had since we left home. He'd been living in Arizona while I was in California. We were close growing up and had missed each other.

Jeff was two years older, but people who saw us together often thought we might be twins. We were both slight of build and fair, with fine-boned features, my brother's most prominent being his soulful eyes. They were that aquamarine shade of blue, while mine were dark-blue steel. He wore his hair long with straight bangs combed loosely over his forehead, a bow to the British Invasion that had changed everything.

In addition to the haircuts and clothes, our ideas and politics were being invented all over again, too. He was a maverick, a musician, an artist, and a sage. Some would describe him as the most irreverent person they knew. He was a wry humorist, a budding comedian. It was difficult not to laugh in his presence over some off-handed remark or unique way in which he viewed any number of situations in front of him. He could fire off detailed pencil sketches, rich with political satire, while holding up his end of an ongoing conversation. He effortlessly painted first-rate in oil and could pick up an instrument and, in no time flat, have it mastered.

When I was around nine or ten, my grandmother Jen bought me an upright piano. My lessons were laborious; my practice painful. My brother, on the other hand, could walk through the room, sit down, and play by ear the exact piece I had just spent hours learning. It drove me nuts at the time. Oh God, though, . . . I adored him.

At Christmas, he would paint the windows from the inside out like a stencil, backwards, with a funny original holiday-themed cartoon. I don't know how he did it. During the summer months, he trained porpoises at a tourist trap in the Hills. The skin on his fingertips was pruned and ragged, but he loved the job. There was always a permanent twinkle behind his eyes and spring to his step. He defied gravity.

In high school, during the R-Day festivities surrounding homecoming, he and his friends created the "er" Club, and Jeff became the mascot, showing up at games wearing a long, skinny red scarf like "the red baron" and smiling for the yearbook photographers. I think it was around this time that he took to calling himself "Ralph," his middle name after my grandfather on my father's side. Odd thing to do at the time really, but sure enough, in short order and for as long as I can remember, all his friends called him Ralph. Who does that? Jeff must have witnessed something or conversed with his grandfather over something important to him to garner such respect for an elder. I like the gesture. I think it demonstrates Jeff's character, too.

He sang tenor in the high school choir and played bass guitar in a garage rock band. They were forever fiddling with names like "The Sarks," after Cutty Sark whiskey, or "Dow Jones and The Industrialists," or "Jeff and the Journeymen." There were two Jeff's in the band then, I think, and I've got a poster on which they called themselves "The Forbidden Children," for which my brother did the artwork. Although it's in pencil, it shows sophistication for his age and the time.

Humor was king; harmony at the helm; and camaraderie thick. The band did "covers" of works by the Dave Clark Five, Gerry and the Pacemakers, the Byrds, and, of course, the Beatles. They wrote and performed their own stuff, too. Having a musician in the family was especially convenient for me, for it gained me exclusive entrée to the clique of older, cuter, and infinitely cooler guys. My girlfriends were "down" with that.

Someone would inevitably have a crush on someone, and I was in the thick of it. By virtue of being the little sister, I could somehow remain just on the fringes, barely visible, whether it was listening to them rehearse, chasing them down the black diamond ski slopes of Terry Peak, running the rapids in our backyard creek, or simply running to pick up the phone and hear the dreamy voice of one of the dudes. Do you remember all the young dudes? I do and they were fine.

I listened to my two brothers witness the birth of rock and roll. They burrowed deep down in the basement, where my older brother, Bill, had a private bedroom and recreation room. He was six years older than me and named William Edgar Magner, Jr., for my father, but physically he took after my grandfather on my mother's side, tall, well over six feet, with the same crop of thick, unruly hair. Bill graduated in 1964, when teens were still drinking and driving and listening to all the Bobbies—Bobby Rydell, Bobby Darin, Bobby Vinton (I know there were more)—along with Fabian and Elvis. Bill's hair was thick with Brylcreem to tame the waves. I would hide out in a cupboard that doubled as the laundry chute and listen, enraptured. When I got caught, tickling was his preferred torture. The phone rang constantly, and up he would fly, taking the stairs two at a time, running off into the night in his tiny blue MG Sprite, Triumph TR6, or Dad's black Austin-Healey.

Both Bill and my father shared a love of exotic cars and speed. My father collected them, albeit one or two at a time, and belonged to a local sports-car club. Our family regularly rallied through the winding hills with other enthusiasts, car tops down, the wind in our hair, linked together like one long string of brightly colored ribbons, laughing at the sky. If the men in the family weren't playing pool in our travel-poster-lined "rec" room telling each other, like Minnesota Fats, to "Rack 'em up," Dad was getting Bill and Jeff to listen to Fats Domino or some new promo while they pored over car magazines and talked music.

My father, William Edgar Magner, Sr., was working both television and radio broadcasting and now "spun platters" on his own show, "The Bill Magner Show," which focused on the big-band sounds of Duke Ellington, Count Basie, and Tommy Dorsey. He especially liked Louis ("Satchmo") Armstrong. Later there would be Henri Mancini and Brazil '66. His album collection was unrivaled, and he had access to all the latest releases. He would bring Judy Garland and Frank Sinatra home for Mom, and at Christmas, sounds of the Norman Luboff Choir and the Ray Coniff Singers filled our home. Comedy albums were the rage then, too. My dad liked Richard Pryor, George Carlin, and a raw talent named Lenny Bruce, but not in the living room.

Dad was the only child of Ralph Beatty and Janet MacCauley Magner. Ralph's mother, Margaret, was married to William E. Magner II, a prominent industrialist, in Duluth, Minnesota, on the shore of Lake Superior. My father's grandfather, the original William E. Magner, had made his fortune in salt, cement, and lime beginning in the early 1880s. He along with his partner, D. G. Cutler, recognized the Twin Ports harbor as an ideal location for their businesses. The Cutler Magner Company utilized cargo space on inbound bulk carriers to transport raw material from the Great Lakes mines to its Duluth salt-processing plant and lime-production facility in Superior. These products were, and still are, used in many ways for paper production, power-plant pollution control, industrial and residential water softening, road stabilization, steel production, and ore processing.

I did not understand the ramifications of the family's power and influence. I just remember seeing the salt cartons that bore the Cutler Magner logo on them and the two families' names scrawled across the docks of that enormous lake, making it into a worldwide shipping port. Their collective vision was strong and innovative enough to carry the company into the present, where it still thrives today. I read recently that it was sold off to a large European enterprise and continues to expand, retaining the Cutler Magner name, but I am as removed from my forefathers, their identities, and this enterprise as a satellite in outer space.

My father's ancestors were from strong Irish stock, hailing from County Cork. I have always felt a deep kinship with the Irish from the moment I set foot on the Ring of Kerry years later. I loved their innate kindness and sense of whimsy—their gift for storytelling and all the inherent pathos attached to it, the Celtic music, the ancient ruins, the resplendent emerald landscapes, the pride, the pubs, the dandelion tea, the works. I like that Irish DNA flows in my veins.

I once met a delightful Irish woman who knew some Magners. She fondly expressed amusement in remembering a Billy Magner to me. She described the family as tavern owners and horsemen, rowdy and spirited. She made me promise to go back again, to look them up, believing they would welcome me with open arms. Perhaps one day.

There is a Castle Magner that now lies in ruin but, in its day, boasted a holy well with special waters to which those from far and wide would come to be healed. The Magner crest and coat of arms bear two lions that face each other. They are raised on their haunches, with an eagle perched on a helmet of armor with a crown at its center.

One particularly intriguing story concerns Robert Magner, from the long line of Magner brothers, who had an intense rivalry with Oliver Cromwell. Cromwell was the lord protector of the Commonwealth of England, Scotland, and Ireland. Cromwell, as lord lieutenant of Ireland, led a campaign in 1649 marked by appalling, merciless massacres. More bloody history. Essentially a willful and powerful dictator, Cromwell came to Ireland during his reign to gloat over his defeat of the Magners and to mock their weakness. As he insultingly tread over Magner graves, Robert heard him utter under his breath, "Well, they are out of the way now." Robert Magner approached him and brazenly stated, "It is easy for living dogs to walk over dead lions." Take that, Cromwell.

Another Magner brother who caught my attention was a Civil War veteran. He was also fluent in Gaelic and Lakota Sioux, which was doubly enthralling to me considering that our family settled and built our home in the heart of Lakota territory.

My great-grandfather's son, Ralph, my father's father, was a tall, slender, quiet man with a shock of corn-yellow hair who wore red-plaid Pendleton shirts, black-leather slippers, and smoked a pipe. He seemed serious to me. He rarely spoke. I was later told that he was a powerful medium, but that he feared and resisted his gift. (Would I love to have a conversation with him now, but maybe he is standing next to me as I write.) His nose was more often than not buried in the financial pages of the *Wall Street Journal*, where he tracked the rise and fall of the stock market and was heavily invested in "blue chips" and commodities. His tobacco smelled like cherry wood. He was never without it.

I was entranced with his subtle dignity and silent ways. I wondered what it was that he pondered so earnestly. What was he thinking about? Or maybe he was listening, receiving information from the other side constantly. Could he tune it out like he tuned us out? I can't recall a single syllable from his lips, or the sound of his voice, only the intermittent click of that pipe against his front teeth, but I loved him. He possessed that "other world" eminence. He knew something I wanted to know.

His wife, my grandmother Janet Macaulay, otherwise known as "Jen," was Scottish born, the eldest daughter of six siblings. Her grandfather, Allen Macaulay, was a sea captain. Her father, George, was a broken man. Her mother, Jessie, died of pneumonia while still young, leaving Jen, the oldest daughter, to help raise the family. I have gorgeous letters that Allen Macaulay, the sea captain, wrote to his children. They were written in a fine hand, dated from different ports of call, and still speak through five generations. He would be lost in turbulent waters off the Cape of Good Hope when he went down with his ship, along with his wife, Kate, who was with him on this final voyage at sea, ironically a trip taken for pleasure.

Jen remained the staunch resolute matriarch of our family until the end. She was stalwart, obstinate, and wove wonderful stories that I wish I had written down. She repeated her ritual of afternoon tea with crackers, and we would gather round her kitchen table with a wooden platter of aged, marbled cheese as a centerpiece while she contemplated a game of canasta, a good smoke, or, if you could prod her to weave a story from the old country, she would wink and begin. My favorite was the one about one of her grandnieces who was a nurse on the fabled *Andrea Doria*, an Italian luxury cruise liner that sank on July 26, 1956, after it collided with the *Stockholm*, a Swedish liner, off the coast of Nantucket Island. Forty-six people died. My grandmother's niece not only survived but came to the aid of a young Italian nobleman, who swept her off her feet and whisked her back to Italy, where they married. It was true love. "One never knows," my mother would whisper, her eyes cast down and away as if she were privy to the dichotomy between this apparent reality and all the polished promise that could crumble and vanish in front of you or never materialize at all. I still believed.

The Macaulay sisters, my grandmother Jen, Isa, and the baby Helen, were lovely and close. Jen and Helen had almost a psychic connection. Helen was dressing for a gala New Year's Eve party one evening when she noticed a spot on her gown. As she rubbed it with cleaning fluid, the dress—along with Helen inside it—ignited and caught fire. She saved herself by throwing on a coat over the flames that engulfed her and rolling in a rug on the floor. In shock and with a wet towel over her head, she ran several blocks to the hospital. When she arrived and looked down, all that remained of her clothing was her shoes.

She nearly died from burns that covered over 90 percent of her petite frame. She went to live with Jen, who helped nurse her back to life. She gradually healed. You had to look hard to see any sign of the scarring, a bare place at the crown of her head and a few faint white seams along her throat and neck. She always carefully applied her makeup and looked perfect, to me, anyway, before I knew. Her life was a testament to her strength, the Macaulay spirit. It must have been that red hair and the Scottish blood coursing through her veins. She was a survivor, too, and lived well into her nineties. After my grandmother died, she and I stayed close and corresponded regularly.

I traced my grandfather Ralph's sister, my great-aunt Merlyn Magner, to Ellis Island in 1911. At the tender age of twenty-two, she immigrated to America and settled on a beautiful lakefront property in Grand Rapids, Minnesota. She was rather enigmatic and eccentric, never married, and had no children of her own.

The story goes that when I was born, my parents were struggling financially. Aunt Merlyn discreetly made them an offer they couldn't refuse, promising that she would pay for all their hospital expenses in exchange for having a namesake. My grandmother wasn't happy about this, as I was about to be named Janet Leslie in her honor, but I retain Janet as my middle name. I've always thought it was somehow poetic that I was bought and paid for. I suppose I was just meant to be a Merlyn, even though I was intimidated by the woman I was named after and often wondered what price, what "pound of flesh," she would eventually extract from me for the privilege of carrying on her name.

Growing up, we would spend idyllic summers with Aunt Merlyn at the lake place, as we called it, where we floated aimlessly around its perimeter in those shiny, big, black rubber inner tubes, our heads thrown back to the sun, drifting. She had a magnificent porch that wrapped all the way around the circumference of the house. Mullioned windows on the lake side turned into natural prisms in the late afternoon light. I thought it was all heavenly, and I didn't know which way to turn first, afraid I might miss something important. My brothers had a card table set up on the sun porch where they would assemble the latest model aircraft carrier or new car. I loved the smell of the glue. We played Parcheesi and Monopoly. Those were golden times.

Cocktails—Rob Roys, Boxcars, and Manhattans—would be served on silver trays for the adults, and we would have chicken-salad sandwiches with fresh-squeezed lemonade on TV trays wherever and whenever we liked. My favorite treat was the orange sherbet from the local creamery. Your slightest wish was my aunt Merlyn's effortless command. She looked like Madame Blavatsky, the Russian occultist and founder of Theosophy, holding court, ready to make it rain roses if she so desired. She seemed that powerful to me.

She loved card games and taught me how to play canasta. For my parents, there would be bridge parties, with crisp, stiff cards from new decks that she shuffled with an automatic machine that I thought was cool. Aunt Merlyn was so immense that she couldn't bend over, so when a card would slip from her hand and drop to the ground, she used a pair of long, silver-engraved tongs to retrieve it . . . very decadent.

I was in awe of her. Spellbound. "Come and stand beside me,

little Merlyn," she would say. I was so shy that I rarely spoke to her. She would gently tug and hug me, and I thought I would disappear forever into the soft, fleshy folds of her body. She smelled like vanilla and omnipotence, and though she rarely opened her mouth to smile, I knew she was thrilled to have a mini Merlyn in the house.

As she was childless, my aunt doted on my father, her nephew, and spoke openly about how Dad was to have the lake place when she was gone. "This will all be your father's one day," she would expound. And my father would shift a little, embarrassed. She would zero in on him and repeat, "Billy, this is your home; it always will be."

The endless days of summer at Aunt Merlyn's would never end, or so we thought. But it was not true. We eventually grew up; she got on in years and grew senile. At the last, her only companion was the attractive young gardener who ended up inheriting everything. Scandalous! All that gardening paid off big time. Who knew? Well, maybe my mother had a hint.

Those memories still remain a treasured postcard from my youth. No one could take her name from me. I was never sure of her legacy, but I tucked it away on a mantel in my mind. We remain connected.

My father, being an only child, was spoiled. He and his parents wintered in Florida, where his cousins owned a small resort in Islamorada, between Key Largo to the north and Key West to the south. There, where they played golf and swam, he grew into a notoriously handsome young man. Later, when he brought us there as kids, all I got was horrible sunburn, and Jeff had a near death encounter with a jellyfish. But there were other wonders.

Dad insisted on driving through the South to absorb this distant and foreign land of rolling green hills with old black folks waving and rocking on their shaded front porches in the Alabama sun. We would smile and wave back like we knew each other. I envied their restful, easy ways, the comfortable naturalness within themselves, while I felt ready to career off into space, ungrounded, able to coalesce right into the ethers. I'd be squashed in the back seat between my two brothers like book ends, them taking pot shots at each other with me, the half-pint referee, in the middle. I'd get pretty cranky at times, but then they would tickle me and make me laugh until I cried, and Mom would intervene and tell us all to behave—a tall order for three young beings who nearly vibrated with kinetic energy and barely contained excitement.

We played games with the billboards by day, looking for hidden words in the signs . . . or hidden signs in the words? By night we anticipated the sight of the orange rooftop of the ubiquitous Howard Johnson Inns that dotted the motorways. They had heated swimming pools and flavored ice-cream sundaes. The car radio was always on, the station changing according to the power and proximity of the local frequency. I would sing or hum along to anything, my tiny rear end bouncing around, my hands clapping, making my mother turn and reach for my hand between the seats.

Dad was interested in magic. Occasionally, he would pull out a purple velvet bag from under the seat at a roadside rest stop, performing some mysterious feat for our entertainment. We were a little band of gypsies ever moving south toward paradise. There would be key lime pie at the other end, and maybe the boys would catch a shark. Yup, they did and brought back the toothy jaw to hang on a bedroom wall. Jeff spray painted it in dark chartreuse to glow in the dark. Gruesome it was.

It was one of the prices paid for this excursion. There had been the blood trailing in the water to lure it in, and although there is no love lost between me and these scary black-eyed predators, I thought it was pretty heartless that they had to drag it back to shore and slowly drown it. Then there were those ugly jellyfish that could suck you up and sting you so bad it made you cry out, swell up like a puffer fish, and kept you out of the water and down for days. But we were together. Salty, sunburned, none the worse for wear. Blissed out.

No matter how much time had passed, Jeff and I were always on the same page when we eventually saw one another again. The night of June 9th, 1972, was no different. When I gazed into those eyes, I was home. We were both children of the 1960s. I knew that he would probably have some decent pot with him.

We anticipated sharing a joint and the ceremony attending it, breaking it out of its secret hiding place in a favored stash box. I prided myself on my expertise in rolling a near-perfect, one-paper joint along with the best of them.

Not all my friends were pot smokers, but it always relaxed me and put things into a softer focus. The added perk was that it gave me the munchies. I did everything under the sun to put weight on my skinny frame in those days. My friends would haul me off to A&W for a pineapple shake or a root-beer float to wash down my chiliburger or pronto pup with mustard. Or I'd ask for an extra scoop of marshmallow sauce on my sundae at Dairy Queen, but in reality nothing worked. My hip-hugger jeans barely hung on my bony hips.

I was a carbon copy of my mother in proportion and measurement. As adults, we were the same height, weight, ring and shoe size. It was simply genetic. Even our voices became identical as I matured. It was the late 60s when Jean Shrimpton and Cheryl Tiegs graced the covers of *Harper's Bazaar* and *American Girl*, but it wasn't yet considered vogue to be super thin. Twiggy hadn't arrived on the scene to surprise us all. I was embarrassed when my brothers teased me publicly, mercilessly, endlessly coming up with newer nicknames, calling me Bones, or Sticks, or Toothpick. Bummer.

Sticks and stones, breaking bones, and all that childhood gibberish aside, the stones and arrows started to sting, not zing by me. It was an awkward, self-conscious phase. I was bothered. But by the time this particular night came around, I had the old *joie de vivre* back. I felt fine, dare I say, happy.

So here we were on a rainy night with the perfect opportunity to kick back, enjoy the house and each other. We took full advantage of it. What could be better than this? I was home for the summer in my old red room with the peonies and Jeffrey's eyes looking back at me. We had nothing but time in front of us and hazy days to burn. Yes, a summer of love, youth on our side, the world at our feet, golden for sure.

By this time Jeff was living in Tempe, near the University of Arizona campus, footloose. But he flew in that first week in June to meet with friends, eat some home-cooked meals, and take measure of his twenty-one years thus far. I had been in California chasing someone else's dreams, living in Los Angeles, which, for a naïve and sheltered girl like me, was akin to living on Pluto. In looking back, it was my innocence that saved me. I was lost and didn't even know it.

My first week in California, I took the advice of a friend in search of cheap dryers at a laundromat in Venice and, with my brother Jeff in tow, was held up at gunpoint by drug addicts who were so high they couldn't even make a clean getaway, pardon the pun. With them waving their guns and knives in our faces, the moment became so surreal that my brother simpered, "Yeah, man, I'm really scared." When they grabbed my purse, I quickly pulled off my rings and handed them over, too. They ran into the alley screaming obscenities at each other while their getaway car broke down.

Jeffrey's eyes met mine. Make no mistake. It was not a movie set. We might have been killed then and there, but our destinies were intertwined in a way that was yet to be revealed. We had literally dodged a bullet in the big bad bright city of the fallen angels. Our escape paved the way for this glorious but ominous day in June.

We began our reunion, nestled together in the familiar safety and security of our home, the house my father had built. Oblivious. We had no way of knowing that we were on the brink of something so staggering that it continues to reverberate . . . a reliable, persistent, defiant, all-together-different echo, ringing down through the canyon walls, spilling over into my present. And so the final hours of our lives as we knew them began to unfold.

4 Jeffrey's Eyes

Home, June 9, 1972

So there I was looking into Jeffrey's eyes that Friday evening in June. They were my eyes. We were twin souls, on a twin journey up until this night, when he put a mirror up to my face and reflected back to me our shared innocence. We were in the family room, the cozy den of the dream house in the canyon. The phone rang. It was Dad calling from the Smiths' cocktail party across the street.

"It looks like the rain isn't going to stop anytime soon, Son. Why don't you move the cars. Pull them up into the driveway."

We weren't alarmed in the least. I remembered being at my best friend Deb's house years before when there had been minor flooding, a common enough event then. Their basement had been trashed, soaked in a muddy mess, and Deb's mom, Evie, lined up pair after pair of her three sons' stiff blue-denim jeans on the front lawn. They were caked with brown soil. She hosed them off and left them outside in the sun to dry . . . a distinct, but distant memory.

In short order, I grabbed the keys to my Mustang, and Jeff, Dad's Thunderbird, as we skipped in unison down the semi-circular drive, hopped in behind the wheel of each car, and pulled up into the curved safety of slightly higher ground. The moisture in the air was palpable. It smelled good and clean, of wet pine needles and fresh-cut grass with a faint hint of lilac.

It hadn't begun in earnest yet. Jeff pulled me onto the front porch and said: "Listen to that. Can you hear that?" Ah, yeah . . . but what was it? It sounded like a dull roar. Where is it coming from, I wondered? "The creek is rising," he said. Yes, we were going to get some water tonight.

We went back to our private reverie of laughter and shenanigans. We decided the folks wouldn't be home for awhile, and we thought it was a good time to roll a joint and lose track of time. Dad had a state-of-the-art stereo system for those days, and we took full advantage of it. It was 1972 and there was a music revolution. My mother's living-room walls were vibrating with Steve Miller Band, the Allman Brothers, Jefferson Airplane, Quicksilver Messenger Service, and the Doors, my personal favorite, the background music of that fateful night. We listened to Jim Morrison wailing soulfully: "What have they done to the earth? What have they done to our fair sister? Ravaged and plundered and ripped her and bit her . . . and tied her with fences and dragged her down."

We plopped down in front of the television with the sound turned off and began the ritual of getting high. The 10 o'clock news was on. I watched Jeff unroll a plastic sandwich bag filled with pot and begin to crumble and clean the seeds and stems with a matchbook cover over a shoebox lid. Then he meticulously glued two zigzag papers together with just the right amount of saliva and seamlessly peppered the loose marijuana into a fine cylinder, with a twist on either end. He winked, handed it to me, and lit a match. I took a long drag, handed it back, and we were off. We both let out a simultaneous and deep, long breath . . . together at last, home sweet home. We could relax now.

While our parents were across the street having cocktails, we were drifting onto a cloud far above it all. But, of course, we weren't really. We were *beneath* the clouds, at ground zero in a deep, dark canyon that, during the light of day, doubled as our backyard. Tonight it held a secret it could not wait to tell. Reality was barging in by the minute. But for the moment our ignorance was truly bliss. Jeff took another long toke and smiled.

I got up and found some of Mom's sandalwood incense to cover the smell of the cannabis. She had a little brass Buddha with a shelf at the center, where the palms of his upturned hands held the cone. We watched the smoke spiral up mixing with the marijuana, doing its work, and glanced at the television screen—small-town newscast, nothing earth shattering or out of the ordinary.

Now Jim was singing, "The days are bright and filled with pain, enclose me in your gentle rain, . . . deliver me from reasons why you'd rather cry, I'd rather fly. . . ." A "crawl" rolled across the bottom of the TV screen that read, "Campers move to high ground." The Crystal Ship was being filled . . . was set to sail.

"So what are you going to do now?" I asked my brother: "Do you plan to stay in Tempe and go back to school or move to Boulder?"

"Nothing too serious yet," he grinned back. "Bum around the Hills, make some music, and paint a little. I imagine."

Me, I was going to work on a serious tan.

The phone rang again, but just as Jeff picked it up, the line went dead. The lights flickered, and we exchanged looks of casual bewilderment. Where were the main power switches if we needed a fuse? "Let's find some candles and light the sconces," I said. The lights went out completely then and weakly flickered back on. The music stopped. The television screen went black. We walked to the front of the house and opened the door. Dad was right. There was water alright.

It was pouring, the sky crackling with electricity and loud claps of thunder. I loved it. I loved storms, weather, the movement of the elements, whether it was wind, rain, or snow. It always made me feel a heightened sense of aliveness. The power went out for the second time and remained down. We quickly stepped back inside, lit another match, this time for light, reached into the dry-sink cabinet by the door, found a candle, and made our way back to the family room. Jeff picked up the phone to see if there was a dial tone yet. Nada. The line was dead. For a moment it was eerily silent. There was a distinct pall in the air, an uncanny foreboding. We would never speak to our parents again.

Our adrenaline was picking up now, and I felt what I thought was merely excitement. My shoulders were high up around my ears. Back to the front of the house, we tiptoed to face the creek and the canyon wall and peer through the large bay window and into that concealed night. I became my brother's shadow, so close he had to tell me, "Mern, give me some breathing room."

Was there a glimmer of fear behind his eyes now? My impulses were telling me to stick close to him. The dogs were hot on our heels. Then we saw water creeping in, seeping up underneath the front door, an unwelcome guest. Jeff looked at me calmly and said, "Go to the bathroom and grab a couple of bath towels." He wanted time to think.

"You're coming with me," I said. I was starting to get scared. This wasn't fun anymore. I couldn't see a thing.

We stumbled down the hall in the dark, like two of the Three Stooges, but without the laughs. We tripped over each other and the dogs, until we got to the linen closet, pulled it open, grabbed whatever our hands made contact with, and reworked our way back to the front of the house. We threw down a crumpled sheet and several towels and clumsily stuffed them under the door.

It had never been this intense before. A loud crack of thunder interrupted our thoughts. I jumped. A streak of lightning flashed ominously. Jeff took my hand, and we carefully made our way back into the den, walking past the French doors at the back of the house. It was then that I caught a look I had never seen on my brother's face. In the flash of lightning, his face had gone slack. It fell forward slightly, and his eyes narrowed as if he were trying to understand or comprehend something, but what?

He took me sternly by the shoulders. His voice lowered an octave. "Mern, the water is rising," he said. "We need to get out of the house and up onto the roof. I don't know if the doors will withstand the pressure."

The roof?. . . what? . . . leave the house? Were we trapped? I shuddered. This new information did not compute. I glanced over his shoulder through the candle glow and realized that the house was engulfed with what appeared to be at least five feet of black water. And it was moving. Waves were forming at the top and lapping just a few feet away. What was happening? Where did it come from? A powerful force wanted in; it wanted in now.

I became incapable of movement. My breath caught. My brain refused to wrap itself around the situation. My mind began to trip. I let out a weird sound. It couldn't be real. I was remembering the time the previous year when Jeff and I were held up at gunpoint in Los Angeles. Surreal is the only word to describe it. Was the water real or a trick of the eye reflecting off the dark interior of the house? We were the fish in a bowl, but the water was on the outside . . . or was it? Suddenly, I knew what scared straight meant.

By this time, my mother's two miniature poodles were barking and starting to freak out. Jeff scooped them up and put them on the kitchen countertop in front of the window near the sink, where they began to slip and slide.

I didn't realize until much later that my brother understood the extreme gravity of the situation and was attempting to save our lives. Then I was in motion. We vaulted up onto the Formica like chimpanzees, with our feet tangling up in the stainless steel sink. Sure enough, Jeff was spot on about the doors. Just as he was opening the kitchen window to begin climbing out of the house, a fissure widened, and with a deafening crack, the French doors split. Water came crashing into the family room and began to spread out over every surface. The last thing I saw as I turned back to look was the refrigerator lying on its side, floating and banging into the breakfast nook. If you could ever say all hell was breaking loose, this was the time.

Jeff grabbed me again firmly, emboldened. It was sobering, horrifying, and dangerous. We exchanged one last eyeball-to-eyeball look, his face inches from mine. "It will be alright Moon," he soothed, "just follow my lead and I will pull you up." I wasn't so sure. With that he turned around, and in one fell swoop, he was standing, his feet positioned on the outside of the window ledge, facing in and hoisting himself up like a gymnast. I panicked.

He had addressed me so lovingly as his kid sister, my big brother and guardian taking control to protect me from harm. But all I could see now were the cuffs of his rain-soaked jeans and his feet disappearing in front of my eyes, with two hysterical dogs jumping and skidding around, their paws not making contact with the smooth linoleum, yelping to high heaven.

Somehow Jeff had made it onto the roof and was now lying flat on his stomach, stretched forward, bending over, looking back through the window, telling me to hand him Cham, the larger and older of the two dogs. She was having none of it. His face was upside down as he reached in and pulled her up by her haunches. "Come quickly, NOW," his voice was urgent. The water was rising fast. There wasn't time. I didn't have the strength to "pole vault" up to the roof the way Jeff had. The water was rushing inward, and I had no leverage to rise up.

A part of me did not want to leave the house at all. I hesitated. Crazy . . . the house represented safety, but I knew I had no choice. I had to make my move. I turned and backed out of the window to position myself for the ascent, to face the house, the roof, Jeffrey's eyes—my lifeline. My skin reeled from the rough, sharp metal frame of the windowsill, which dug into my hands and knees as I slid down into the water.

Water engulfed me. I must have been in shock now because I couldn't feel the temperature of it, which I know was as cold as it was dark, but I was in it. I had placed the other dog in the sink, thinking I would pull her out after me. My fingertips were taut, grasping the rim of that window for dear life.

Then, everything went wrong and the dog was on top of me. I lost my grip and the battle against the current. It felt like the weight of the world was pressing in on me, against the small of my back and shoulders. It was blacker than swirling ink. My brother's face had disappeared. I was getting ready to meet my Maker.

The sky, the water, the night merged and darkened as if God had pulled some giant switch backstage on this little world play. The curtain fell, and we were all on our own. What was once our patio and backyard, a safe haven where we had spent endless hours lying in the grass filled with joy, was now a mammoth tide of untold horrors.

Within seconds, this dense black wall slammed into us and tore me from the intimate safety of my brother's outstretched arms and the anchor of my home. Carub, my mother's chocolate-colored miniature poodle, became hysterical and began to shake and claw at my face and chest and push my head down under the surface. I started to choke and instinctively pushed her away to get my head above the water again. Then realizing what I had done, I began to look frantically for her and Jeff, but it was so dark, with only intermittent flashes of lightning from above.

I thought I saw the top of Jeff's head bobbing in the water just out of my reach, but how had he gotten back into the water? Had he been overcome, or was he coming after me? Was I imagining that he was there with me, or was he long gone, severed from me, our separation complete and final? If I hadn't known better, I would have thought we were in high seas, shipwrecked. And then what I thought was the top of his head was just more illusion. I didn't see either dog.

I never saw my brother alive again.

Water was everywhere now. The sound of thunder rumbled across the heavens so loudly, it was as if Zeus were beating his own chest. Strobes of lightning flashed across the sky. I was tumbling through darkness, just trying to keep my head above the water, but it kept trying to take me, pulling me, pushing me down, and swallowing me whole.

The last time my head surfaced, I caught a glimpse of my parents on the rooftop of the neighbors' house. The last thing I saw before going down for what I knew was my "final count" was my mother, teetering on a rain gutter in the sky, looking like she was standing at the water's edge, her outline barely visible, but all too real, an inept savior, a fleeting angel . . . reminding me of the way women in my family seemed to appear during a crisis, as my grandmother had when I was a child, only to then vanish . . . how could my mother recover from this?

One hand clutched her chest and that fragile, damaged heart. She buckled to her knees, collapsed, and cried out, "Bill, the children." Pointing in my direction, she saw me, struggling for breath, rushing past her in the current. She was watching me and possibly watching Jeff, as well. She was watching her children struggle in that darkest of night and drown.

I could barely, faintly hear my father calling out, straining above the din, "Grab onto something and float." But I couldn't respond. Debris was everywhere, like weapons indiscriminately mingling with pieces of broken homes, broken cars, and broken lives. There were people, too, caught up and being pulled along as I was, gulping for and desperately seizing the air, reaching out for something, anything, to stay afloat, to survive.

But there was nothing to hold on to. It was impossible. There was no way out. The strongest Olympic swimmer could not have navigated out of those waters. They were too strong, too violent. They were swollen and merciless. We were all lost. It felt Biblical. So this was how the world will end.

I don't know how long I was actually under the surface of the water. I could feel my lungs filling up with fluid, and I knew I was running out of time. I was dying. I was watching the news ten minutes ago, and now I was dying. Strange, I wasn't frightened now. Then it happened. I ran out of oxygen.

I wasn't breathing anymore, and it was a relief. I began to float into a kind of warm knowing, a liberated level of being. My life, my body, this nightmare was behind me, and it didn't matter. Nothing did. On the contrary, I was at peace. There was no pain or panic, no more choking, no clinging to or desperation for life. I felt an ineffable, absolute oneness, a calm certainty that I was home. On that night around 10:25 P.M., I was floating above a canyon filled with death and destruction in total bliss. I was dead. Drowning was another baptism. I was born again into pure consciousness. I thought earlier that day I knew what it felt like to be free. I wasn't even close.

I had no attachment to my body whatsoever, and in fact, I felt as if I had slipped off a tight garment. There was an "ahh moment," an epiphany. I was elated. I was dead, but I was still alive. How could this paradox be? Yet, it was more than natural. Being born into the world felt like falling into another kind of sleep, a long dream, and dying, like waking up. I had touched a deep and simple truth, the secret held in the canyon this revelatory night, and it contained a profound remembrance. I was love itself. Holy Mother.

Then, just as I was becoming comfortable in this newfound freedom, I was abruptly jolted back into my body. My arm and side slammed up against a shake-shingled rooftop of the new two-story condominiums that were being built on the creek bed just across the highway from our home. In what I can only describe as a Herculean instant, I instinctively pulled myself up onto the slope of the rain-soaked wood, retching and throwing up water and mud and bits and pieces of God knows what.

My arm was scraped and bleeding, but not bad. My side hurt.

I was on my belly now, clinging to the slanted platform that had become my life raft. I could feel every splinter of every square-shaped piece of tile, smell the damp, dead bark. I could barely lift my head . . . it felt like a thirty-pound bowling ball, crooked on the stem of my neck. I always wore my hair long and straight, usually in a ponytail or high single braid down my spine to my waist, but this night, my hair was loose, and as I somersaulted through the deluge it had gathered twigs, leaves, and even a branch or two. My head tilted to one side from the sheer weight.

I pictured myself as Medusa crowned by nature. I let my head fall and pressed my cheek tightly into the side of the roof and closed my eyes, bracing for the inevitable onslaught that would reclaim me. It was so cold now. I wore the top of a two-piece swimsuit covered with a T-shirt and a pair of tattered cutoffs. I was barefoot. My T-shirt clung to me like a heavy second skin stretched out over my thin frame. I was five feet six inches, weighed around 104 pounds soaking wet, and had small bones. You could place your thumb and forefinger around my wrist and still slide three more fingers into the space left over. But I felt like I weighed a thousand pounds as I became one with my body again. I was stunned, and it must have taken me a moment to compose myself.

Even though I now had a perch, it was precarious at best, and I still believed the worst was coming. I was in shock. How can the mind comprehend homes folded up like paper dollhouses, fragments floating by, some with neighbors, people you knew, you grew up with, you babysat for, your friends attached to them, clinging to life, screaming and gasping for breath as I had been seconds before? But I didn't see any of their faces then; I couldn't look for long. I shut my eyes so tightly that I forgot to breathe again, but I couldn't shut out the sound. The sky had opened and was belching thunder. Timber was exploding, voices were crying out for salvation.

I tried to imagine the beautiful void I had glimpsed. I would wait. This was Hell. I knew better—Heaven existed. There was a place beyond this plane where I belonged and everything made perfect sense. There were no questions there. Before you could form one, the answer was simply known, and along with it came a peace so profound that it indeed surpasses understanding. Yes, it was love straight up, unconditional. It was real. Cling to it.

My body had become a stranger to me, a frightened, needy companion. It felt disconnected to this stark reality that I found myself in. It didn't understand what we were doing here or why, but it cleaved to me like a captive prisoner whose survival depended on my staying put. I would never uncover the pervasive mystery of life or the why of this moment in time, except that it was happening and I couldn't change it. Why do we attempt to survive at all costs, against all odds . . . this instinct to be alive no matter what?

And why was I steadily making my way up the incline of this shake-shingle roof to get to the top . . . to safety? What was holding me back from simply waiting there for the inevitable end that would surely come or from just letting go, back into the lull of the tender twilight of the dying. I knew now that life this night was a dream; the nightmare and dying and leaving my body had birthed me into real life, my real home, the pure love I knew I was made of.

And my present home, what of it? Where was it? Had it too given way to this magnificent madness? Had it floated by? Was the rest of my family already there, on the other side, waiting for me, watching this scene play out inside a darkened theatre like a preview trailer on a three-dimensional movie screen? Yes, after tasting death, I was tempted to swallow it whole again. I wanted to submerge myself back into that gentle, pale, elusive escape and away from this nebulous gloom.

A kind of homesickness began to set in, on every level you can imagine, for my family, my home, my former self, what lie beyond. I had no doubt that this structure that was yet unfinished and supporting me would, in a matter of time, collapse and be washed away. I still thought this was the end for us all in this unholy place and time. Nothing would ever be the same again. I wasn't frightened anymore, except for the pain. I knew what was coming. It could be any second, minutes . . . time ceased to have meaning. But I continued to climb to the highest point near a bubble-shaped skylight and waited.

As the night deepened, my body became colder and colder until finally I was sitting on my haunches upright in a fetal position, my knees to my chest and my T-shirt pulled over my head like a kind of tent. My teeth were chattering loudly and uncontrollably; yet, I heard some people in a tree nearby. I couldn't make out much, except that at one point they yelled out to me, "Are you alright?"

"I'm okay. Let's pray." I shouted back. Or did I? I only heard the rage of the flood in my ears and could feel my heart beating furiously against my scrunched up thighs.

I thought about my family. Where was my brother? He was always my champion, my hero. Was he hurt or suffering? Did he die trying to save me? What happened to my parents? I wouldn't know until the next day, when I saw that the house they were standing on was gone, that they, too, were caught up in the raging waters.

Could those bodies and people who had called out for help in the night in fact have been my beloved family, their lives hanging in delicate balance as I huddled there exposed? Did my mother succumb to another heart attack, and did my father, ever her knight in shining armor, once again try to save her as she ebbed away from him? I know he was holding her until the end, but what end? Did he, too, become separated from her, like Jeff and I had, helplessly searching in the heaviness that was that night to then be torn from each others' arms, slipping away to struggle and die alone? Did they in fact float for a time?

No, I think not. This thing was too brutal. It was not the steady, harmless current of a stream, but more the pent-up rage of retribution. I thought that God was angry that night, mad at me, at the world. Hadn't this been the case when this identical scenario played out thousands of years before?

When I looked up, the sky was black and then filled with white fire. The sound of the thunder made my body start in fright. The heavens had opened, and the combination of all four elements spewed forth . . . a deluge of rain, wind, and fire until the earth beneath me cried out. The gods were spitting and yelling at us, all in unison. I felt miniscule there by myself, so alone. My safe beautiful home just across the way was a dream that ended. I prayed to face death again bravely and asked to be forgiven for whatever we had done to bring this wrath upon us. It was all too much for my nineteen years to fathom. It was unspeakable, irretrievable. It was final.

By now my teeth were clenched and my body was convulsing from the cold. When would I hear the sound of wood splintering beneath me and the piercing clap of shattered glass rushing through windows and doors that would not hold back this torrent of utter destruction? Would I fall through the ceiling and be knocked unconscious with the force of heavy beams coming down on top of me? I prayed that it would be quick and that the water would find me again so that I could quietly slip into that sweet slumber, the ultimate surrender, death.

I wasn't looking out over the side of the rooftop. My body was in lockdown. I had pulled my arms out of the sleeves of my T-shirt and wrapped them tightly underneath and around my legs, my head bent forward, my neck and Medusa head protruding out of the top of my shirt. My body became my armor. I was sure I was in a losing battle. My leg, arm, and back muscles became the walls of an invisible fortress against the storm. I exhaled long and deep breaths for the second time that night, not in jubilation with Jeff serenely at my side when it began, but in survival mode here in the dead of night, breathing down into my chest cavity to create a furnace for warmth. My T-shirt, a thin, wet cotton tent, became the barest boundary, the only thing between me and the rest of the world, this infinite and terrible night.

I rocked back and forth, soothing my nerves, and began to hum. The minutes turned into hours and the hours into prayers until at last it was dawn.

Statistics

"Water . . . traveled at 10 times the speed and strength of any previous recorded flood in the area. . . . Streams had swelled as an unheard-of 10 to 15 inches of rain fell on the parched, non-porous land. Water and debris poured down the hills and canyon walls, ripping through every bridge, every house along the banks, widening as much as 8 miles in their sweep. . . . With the dawn, National Guard soldiers guarding the roads and neighborhoods of destroyed property, a search began. There would be 233 bodies discovered in coming weeks; five more would remain buried forever. Three thousand people had been injured; more than 1,300 homes destroyed."
—*Rapid City Journal*, 9 June 2002

"President Nixon issued his federal disaster-area declaration for four counties on Saturday afternoon. Federal funding, private donations and thousands of volunteers poured into the area as Black Hills communities began to dig out from the tragedy. Federal aid totaled $170 million, including a $48 million HUD urban renewal grant that enabled the city to buy property in the flood plain and move owners to higher ground. A quickly-formed disaster foundation began administering $1.4 million in private donations from all over the country."
—*Deadwood Magazine*, May/June 1996

"Record flows were reported on Rapid, Battle, Bear Butte, and Boxelder Creeks. On June 9 [1972] a stationary front, with moderate southeast surface flow, moved through high pressure aloft. A strong flow of warm, moist air near the surface fed the storms and anchored them against the

Hills for six to eight hours. An average of six inches of rain fell with up to 15 inches reported. Rainfall intensities of two to six inches/hour were common. Canyon Lake breached, adding to the wall of water that poured through Rapid City. Flow on Rapid Creek in Rapid City was estimated at 50,000 cfs. After the flood, 750 acres near Rapid Creek were designated as a floodway. 238 deaths and $164 million in damages were reported."
–National Weather Service, 2010

Merlyn Magner at about the age when her father invited her to "come into the water." Merlyn Magner collection

Merlyn's mother, Norma Elizabeth Anderson Magner. Merlyn Magner collection

Norma Elizabeth Anderson and William E. Magner, Sr., on their wedding day, January 6, 1946. Merlyn Magner collection

(opposite) William E. Magner, Sr., worked in television broadcasting in Flint, Michigan, until the family moved to South Dakota in about 1959. Merlyn Magner collection

*Janet ("Jen")
Macaulay Magner,
Merlyn's paternal
grandmother, was
the matriarch of
the family and
helped bury the
Magners who died
in the flood.* Merlyn
Magner collection

*Bill Magner, Jr., as
a high-school senior
in 1964.* Rapid City
Central High School
collection

*Jeffrey Magner
in a 1968 high-
school photograph.*
Merlyn Magner
collection

The Magner house in Rapid City in 1967, five years before the flood. Merlyn Magner collection

Merlyn Magner landed on the roof of this condominium after the flood waters swept her from her home. Jeffrey Magner painted this image. Merlyn Magner collection

These ruins are all that remained of one of the condominiums after the flood. Perry Rahn collection

Downstream from the ruined condominium, fallen trees, wrecked cars, and the remains of houses littered Rapid Creek. Perry Rahn collection

These damaged houses stood on the floodplain of Rapid Creek in what was the Meadowbrook area. Perry Rahn collection

This United States Geological Survey gauge along Route 44 registered a peak discharge of thirty-thousand cubic feet per second during the flood. Perry Rahn collection

After the flood, searchers marked houses with an S if it had been searched, and an X if it was condemned. United States Geological Survey collection

The force of the floodwaters stacked these cars one on top of another. United States Geological Survey collection

In Memory Of

WILLIAM EDGAR MAGNER
November 30, 1920   June 9, 1972

NORMA E. MAGNER
June 24, 1924   June 9, 1972

JEFFREY RALPH MAGNER
March 10, 1950   June 9, 1972

Funeral Services and Burial
June 17, 1972   Duluth, Minnesota

Memorial Services
Campbell-Paula Funeral Home
7:30 P.M.   Thursday, July 20, 1972

Officiating Clergyman
Rev. Dan Leighton

Services Conducted By
Campbell-Paula Funeral Home
Rapid City, South Dakota

Music
Organist .... Zona White

All are victims of the Rapid City flood
of June 9, 1972.

A memorial service for the Magners was held in Rapid City on July 20, 1972. Merlyn Magner collection

Merlyn Magner in 1974, about two years after the flood.
Merlyn Magner collection

Merlyn Magner, right, and her friend Vickie Plummer on the ski slopes in the Black Hills. Merlyn Magner collection

From left, Heidi Becker, Catherine Bachman, and Carol Hayes at Merlyn's wedding in December 1983. Merlyn Magner collection

From left, Merlyn Magner, Catherine Bachman, and Pam Lester on location in Africa. Merlyn Magner collection

Bill Magner, Jr., and his wife at their home in Thailand. Merlyn Magner collection

All that remains of the Magner home in Rapid City is this hearth. Merlyn Magner collection

The former site of the Magner home is now a park. The shrubbery that once grew in front of the house marks the location. Merlyn Magner collection

Merlyn Magner on Zuma Beach near Malibu, California.
Merlyn Magner collection

5 The Day after the World Ended

As dawn approached, I realized that at last the storm was over. I was alive. I had miraculously survived, but how, why? Time disappeared along with the night. The sky had quenched her thirst and was pacified for now. All was still. I thought of the philosopher's story of when a tree falls in the forest. If there is no one there to hear it fall, does it make a sound? Had the world ended? The one I knew had. I would be split between two new worlds now; the one that I inherited in the light of this new day and the ethereal one I knew existed in another kind of light that I could not now see, find, or feel. I had left it behind in the night.

Then I heard a sound. It was like a foghorn coming out of the ocean mist, only not as loud. I stuck my head out from underneath my flimsy refuge and peeked over my shoulder. The muscles around my neck and eyes were tight, as if all night they had been clenched in a fist. Off in the distance, I could just make out a series of large, flashing red lights moving methodically, closer and closer. It looked armored, like me. Was it a boat, a tank? Had the reserves come? Absurd, but I could believe it was a war zone. The light of dawn was filtered, unfocused. Something about that morning made you want to squint. My eyes felt like tiny black casings from a discharged BB gun, spent, inert.

What was real here? Could I trust my own gauge for this new reality? My perception was askew. I didn't recognize myself anymore. Everything had changed. Everything was different now. Who was I? In the new landscape I occupied, I had become a frightened girl child awaiting rescue. The day before I had been a confident young woman sure of her path in life, going forward. What of the transcendent self I'd glimpsed beyond my body when I had died? How would I reconcile myself between these two diverse and complex realities? What of the self-assured colt, at the gate, valiant and ready to bolt? . . . vanished, history. And in her place was an injured, enigmatic creature separated from all she knew and held dear. I couldn't make a sound.

From then on, all would be divided . . . into before and after. Overnight I'd become Lancelot or Perceval, a naïve and bungling knight wandering off in search of the Holy Grail. I was wounded. All around me was the aftermath of a battle. I'd lost my kingdom and my court. My tribe was gone . . . nothing left but smoke and ash.

The road in front of me was concealed just as it had been the previous night when we had dared to see into it, to understand it from inside our fortress of dreams—impenetrable then as now. My vision blurred; my heart pierced. The Darkness had kept her secrets intact. Nothing was clear or meaningful. The maps I needed did not exist. Truth was myth. I'd lost my compass. My dear companions were all presumed dead behind me on the road I thought I had recognized. It, too, was past, over.

A beacon of hope moved towards me on the horizon. The National Guard had come to search, rescue, and recover. My breathing became more measured now. With the breaking sunrise, I could see some people in the treetops adjacent to me. I couldn't speak, but at least the Guard knew we were here. Yes, there were survivors. And I was one of them. Rescue was imminent. A new day, a new play was about to begin.

My surroundings resembled the abandoned set of *Escape from New York*, a bad piece of fiction. All was gray and carbon tinged, wet, and foul. There were spirals of smoke in the air where fires were burning out of control. It smelled like gasoline and heating oil. And there was something else. Yes, strange, yet distinctly unmistakable, the air smelled of death. Those who awoke that dreadful morning in the city could tell you how it smelled. The combination of the earth being torn asunder by a billion tons of water crushing everything in its wake and the randomness of what was laid waste in its path was unimaginable.

This was another country. I hadn't seen this place before. One side of a street would be decimated, the other unscathed and perfectly intact. Trees were uprooted. Homes were smashed like miniature erector sets cast aside by bored children. Roads were littered with lumber, steel, and pipes—homes turned inside out. I closed my eyes again, bunched up like a fist. If I could shut out this new horror, perhaps I could switch to another reality as swiftly as this one had changed.

Then, I heard the voice of a man with authority shouting out to someone in a commanding way. I also recognized the white Jeep of my friend, the architect Richard, who had built our home. He spotted me, too. The good guys were here.

I heard muffled conversation below me. It was only a matter of time before a concerted effort would get me off this rooftop and onto solid ground, whatever that meant. The water appeared to have receded. I surveyed my immediate surroundings. Yes. I was alone on top of the second story of a building. Impossible. I looked down through the broken skylight next to me and caught a glimpse of "safety," my ground zero. I felt dizzy, disoriented, and cold. The as-yet-uninhabited rooms on both floors, some-one else's dream house, had been destroyed.

Everything happened in slow motion. I was unplugged, sepa-rated, suspended. A house divided between two dimensions. I couldn't know then that I wouldn't come back into my body for decades. Denial, my old and trusted friend, became a powerful ally and useful device for a mind overwhelmed. No, it would not fail me now. A switch had flipped in my brain to protect me from all this. In less than ten hours, I had gone from carefree abandon and hopeful anticipation of a bright future to a still, dead calm without resources.

I heard I was completely naked when they pulled me from the mud and the madness, half dead, with a silver bracelet, such a delicate trifle, dangling from my hand. I read later in a book called *The Children's Blizzard*, by David Laskin, that those found scattered dead in the snow were partially clothed, in fact appeared to have torn at their coats and scarves to free themselves. The phenomenon is associated with hypothermia, in which a victim's nerves adversely feel as if they are on fire and so he or she begins to pull off clothing, a theory I initially rejected, not wanting to believe it because it was just too fantastic, extraordinary, not to mention deeply embarrassing. Now I must concede that there may be a grain of truth in it. I have learned that the mind shields us from much that is more than we can bear. I even considered that the sheer force of the water may have stripped me.

I looked across the highway for the home where my parents had been stranded just hours ago. The house had disappeared, leaving a flat, bare cement foundation where it had once stood. The enormity of this sight did not register. I did not see any survivors, no signs of life, but my eyes were bits of shrapnel now, my reality splintered. Where was I? Did it have a name . . . ? Our home, from which Jeff and I had only hours before attempted escape, was still there, although it was ravaged. Suddenly, I was standing on shifting sand, and a step in any direction would make me topple and plunge into another unknown. The once familiar terrains, both inside and out, had altered forever.

I still didn't know what had happened. It didn't matter. Nothing mattered. In the cold dim light of the morning of June 10th, everything was stark, washed out, barren—empty, gutted, and numb. The same way I felt inside. A small group of men stood directly beneath me, all staring up at me, talking and working a kind of sign language in my direction. I think they wanted me to find a way to breach the glass dome next to me, to widen the opening so that they could begin their ascent up and through it. Nope, I was glued to the spot.

Mick Jagger and his wild horses couldn't have gotten me to make a move. This rooftop, this precarious perch, had been my lifeline for the last nine hours. I would sit this out a while longer. The truth is I couldn't have moved if I'd wanted to. My free will wasn't working worth a damn either. All my systems seemed to be short circuited. I might as well have been back in the womb, in water.

I heard glass shattering, and sure enough, the skylight next to me was cracking to make way for the cables that would snake their way up through the ceiling, wrap themselves around me, and, pulley-fashion, bring me down through two stories of a demolished townhouse. I was suspended in air, space, and time. Someone would have to coax me down. My limbs, my mind, my senses didn't trust movement of any kind. I trusted nothing.

A kind and sturdy man told me that everything would be alright. Those were Jeff's exact words; was it just last night? Again, I wasn't so sure. Could I get that in writing?

"Just put your arms around my neck and hold on to me," the man said. I'd been holding on for hours. How was I to let go now and hold on to this stranger connected to this thin black line of wire suspended in more thin air between jagged shards of glass and just free fall some thirty feet?

Where was Jeff? His arms were supposed to be around me. Where was my brother? My father? He once told me, that little girl in the flounced swimsuit at the pool, that he wouldn't let go, told me so patiently, so endearingly, to "come into the water."

Where was my mother? Dead? Where the hell was I? . . . somewhere between the darkest night and the dawn of . . . what . . . ?

My fingers were red and stiff. My body was still in tight lockdown. I must have seemed to my rescuer like the dead weight of a reluctant corpse. What felt like rigor mortis was settling into my body, but I was still breathing, barely. Before I could slow down the whole process to "process" it, down we flew through the air and onto terra firma, where I was placed into the arms of Richard. In retrospect, I think he was there to assess the damage to his latest design project, the spec property that had effectively saved my life. He was probably quite taken aback to see me huddled up there in the sky . . . both of us mystified, stupefied. And, of course, his beloved mother lived just across the street from us.

It must have been around 7 A.M. It was quiet. Richard had probably said, "Yes, I know her. I am a friend of the family." He lowered me into the familiar smell of the leather seat in his white Jeep, my white knight who threw his brown leather jacket loosely around my slender shoulders. His face was ashen. I was a ghost. How do you speak to one?

I don't remember stopping at my parents' home for any kind of inspection or assessment. It practically felt like a sacrilege to talk anyway. I don't remember looking back around at my neighborhood at all after the initial glance towards my cul-de-sac. We just made a slow, wide U-turn and headed back towards the city, or what was left of it. I can only imagine how I must have looked . . . a barefoot, skinny waif, soaked to the bone and mute, shut down, the object of pity.

Had I uttered a sound yet? My mind spoke one word, "No."

Richard silently drove me to the house of a friend of my mother's, Mary Carlin, who lived on West Chicago Street where I grew up. I have little recall of this time, but I imagine that she tried to feed me, lead me into a hot shower, and give me dry clothes. She was always so kind, a gentle soul. I heard the radio droning on with all the latest bulletins. Mary spoke to me . . . or tried. Did I hear the words, "get you to the hospital?" But her face and voice were coming from a long dark tunnel, far away in another galaxy.

Something flipped over in my mind suddenly, and all I wanted to do was move. I had to get out. I had no destination, only nerves for gasoline. I set out on foot and began to wander. I moved . . . from familiar house to familiar house, while friends periodically kept track of my whereabouts, I guess. Probably as long as I wasn't behaving too bizarrely, or appearing outwardly hurt, their consensus was, "Just let her be. She will come around sooner or later and settle down." Yeah, I came around, but I never quite settled.

So began a pattern that permeated my being and fueled the engine that drove my every waking breath, becoming my only comfort. I would be in ceaseless, continuous motion for the rest of my life.

My older brother Bill, William Edgar, Jr., who was in the Air Force, was summoned from overseas. He was completing his second tour of duty in the Vietnam mess and hopped a plane immediately to come home on emergency leave. He would know what to do, I told myself. Somehow I got to his wife's house, where the phone was ringing nonstop. She looked sedated, and I couldn't speak her language either. I "checked out" of there and wandered some more.

Life can truly turn on a dime. In one night, Bill's and mine were blown to smithereens in the bang heard halfway round our world. I had been swept away, stranded on a rooftop in a flash flood; our house and home had become a forsaken tomb; and our family was missing. The worst was yet to come.

I remember sitting in a therapist's office years later, hearing him say, "Well, the worst has already happened." Really? For those left behind, this couldn't be further from the truth. He was wrong, dead wrong. Back then, I had not even begun to grasp the impact the flood would have on my life. I did not know how the tragedy had impaired my innate ability to trust and allow love in. Forget about forgiving almighty God and myself for surviving—my family, wherever they were, were not here, in this purgatory that had enveloped me. I knew they were together.

Yes, the event was over, but the repercussions had only begun. I wondered if Bill ever looked at me thinking, "Why you? How did you make it out alive?" Would he have been different had we all perished? I often thought about how different our lives would have been had they all lived. But that "what-if" thinking can really make for madness. I would become a conundrum to myself and all those around me along the way. I could feel people staring and whispering, pitying me.

The toll on Bill, too, and our relationship would be immeasurable. When my brother arrived in Rapid City in a few days time, shock was written all over his face, but he took the situation in hand. He was the man and had my back. We both understood the unspeakable. No words flowed forth. His task was combing the makeshift morgues for the bloated bodies of our lost family.

My friend Rhonda Buell had volunteered at the local courthouse after the flood to issue permits granting people access to the then-restricted flood zone. She told me later that it sounded pretty tough, but she agreed to do it. So many volunteers helped out where there was a need, many of them truly good people, but they would stand in stark contrast to the malignant paradoxes that lay in the days ahead.

It turned out that all those who approached her table in the courthouse shared a common reason; they were looking for loved ones. She said, "Mern, I didn't turn anyone away." The National Guard needed room to work and prevent looting and further damage to property. In the room where she sat, Rhonda had a view of the list of names of victims as they were being identified. "To my heartbreak, I saw them write your dad's name on the board," she told me. "Was it my imagination, or was his name the first on the list?" she wondered.

I have concluded that because of my father's TV exposure, being in everyone's living room night after night, he was merely recognized immediately, but I don't really know where he died, or who found his body. He was already identified by the time Bill got there. His body was on the floor of a church, lined up with some of the over two hundred others who lost their lives that night, who had been brought there for purposes of identification and to be claimed by family members. Bill identified Jeff a few days later, as I recall. I was at a class reunion years ago when someone made the off-hand remark that the only way they "knew" it was my brother was because of the Pisces belt buckle he wore on his flood-soaked jeans. How she knew this inside information I'll never know. I wanted to throw my glass of ice water into her smiling . . . yes, smiling . . . face.

My mother's body would not be found for weeks. We accompanied three caskets to Duluth for funeral services, but one of them was empty. While we were in flight, her remains were located miles away on the other side of town. She was finally identified through her dental records. I know that I was told this. It is embarrassing when people ask me where my mother's remains are now. I have to be perfectly honest; the sad truth is I have no clue. How can this be?

Over a decade ago, when Bill got up to shave one morning and dropped dead of a heart attack in Thailand where he eventually retired, it brought me to my knees. He would always be so far from home. I was later told that he had too many people in his heart. It can get really crowded in there. That was something I could understand. But there is more I need to tell about the time after the flood.

The house was a complete loss, but it seemed so inconsequential. Dad had no mortgage insurance at the time, so Bill and I paid off the house with the life insurance and abandoned the now-empty shell. It was completely devoid of the life it once held. The spirits of my dismembered family had deserted it. It was a dismal and forlorn reminder of what had once been a safe and happy harbor in every other imaginable storm in life.

But it was also holy ground. It was the place where my family turned and walked through a different door. I had, too—I'd opened the door to follow them, but I was turned back. I had unfinished business to attend to. If I had known then how much was stacked up, lying in wait, I'm not sure I'd have made it off that rain-soaked roof after all.

Disasters create opportunists, and the flood in Rapid City was no exception. It brought out the vultures—people both known and unknown to me—who saw a way to accumulate more or turn a profit from tragedy. And so began a most extraordinary phenomenon at the house my father built. What was left of it was systematically stripped bare like a discarded carcass in what was now a wasteland. The Franklin stove, shipped from New England, the centerpiece of our den, was hauled off by thieves in the night. What was left of my family's belongings began to disappear, piece by bloody piece, until even the light switches and fixtures had vanished.

I didn't give a rat's ass about these things and simply shrugged my shoulders when, during the few times we returned to seek out a picture, take stock, or find some form of comfort to try to make sense of that night, we discovered that the hardware of our house had gone missing. Of course, none of the "material" mattered, has never mattered; it's all just so much stuff; but oddly and sadly over the years, more and more of my life would eventually revolve around picking up the pieces of the lost fortunes of my disappearing family. It was the cheap and misplaced priorities surrounding these circumstances that injured me. Where the house stood was consecrated ground to me. It belonged to no one . . . what little remained there was left to God. Now, other players huddled behind the curtain on this stark stage, directed by shadows, acting out in ways that were so bizarre, it defied understanding. Certain things scarred my soul and shook me to the marrow. One day I would walk into a "friend's" house and see my mother's Mason jars all lined up on the kitchen shelf, perfectly clean and polished like they had been sitting there for years. Or one of her handbags would be lying on the countertop, like she had just dropped by for a cup of coffee.

Sometimes I would drive by the house in the canyon and see familiar cars—cars belonging to people we knew, who were rummaging and digging in the mud for scraps of whatever the flood waters hadn't taken. My family wasn't enough? Now it was open season on the spoils?

It always amazed me when I spoke of my loss. Sometimes the first thing people wanted to know was what happened to the property, who owned it now, where was all the stuff? Why were other people preoccupied with the temporal things of my life? No one ever said: "Tell me about your father. What was your mother like? Damn, you must miss your brother. How are you holding up?" I don't blame anyone, though. What does one say? It's easier to talk about the stuff, I guess, but, believe me when I say, talking about the love goes a long way in healing the wounds. I wanted people to know my family existed, that they loved me, and that I deeply loved and missed them. I wanted people to know, profoundly, truly, that love is all that is left to any of us in the end. Love. The rest is all so much illusion we manifest and manipulate.

While no one breathed a word about my true loss, great energy was spent defiling and desecrating the altar of my family's home. All around town, sacking the remains of family homes became a dishonorable and diabolic pastime. No, nothing in this new world I inhabited was sacred.

It was one thing that strangers unknown to me had foraged through my shell-shocked home and made off with "valuables" and whatever else wasn't bolted down. One does not have high expectations of strangers. But I did hold my friends to a higher standard, and I was appalled to know that some of my so-called friends—people known to me and my family—were out stealing what remained of our personal effects. It was so unfathomable at the time that I simply couldn't address it then and there, but I have never forgotten.

How I wished my father's house had washed clean away that night along with all the dreams it held . . . realized or imagined. Did they think I didn't notice? The truth is, had they simply asked me I probably would have said, "Go ahead, if there is something in that pile of mud you can't live without, have at it, knock yourselves out." To pretend they were somehow invisible to me was just beyond my comprehension. It was stunning, shameful, and deeply wounding to me and the memory of my family.

There was the friend who collected money for clothes for me, calling it the Merlyn Relief Clothing Fund. She put together a tidy sum, proceeded to buy herself a brand-new wardrobe, . . . and then she was gone. There was another adult who sought me out the very next day and pushed a $100 bill into my hand for my Mustang. I was dazed and confused enough at the time that I simply stood there. He told me the car was worthless, trashed now, and he was doing me a big favor by taking it off my hands. The next week he was driving it around town.

I had no reference point for any of this behavior. I was already in a state of shock and profound denial, so tipping the scales even further did not register. I did not react nor respond to these grisly episodes . . . not then. I was an innocent lamb to the slaughter, a bona-fide textbook victim. When Bill left to go back overseas, never to return to the States, no one would ever have my back again. I wasn't talking to God yet. The blatant unconsciousness of it blows me away to this day. All these episodes gave new meaning to the word "disgrace" for me. While these conniving plunderers were pillaging and looting the spoils of my lost family, my brother and I were using the insurance money to pay off the mortgage on a gutted, noninhabitable bunker of sorrow.

I did manage to retrieve a few items on those few desolate trips back inside with my brother. He appeared despondent with a kind of despair I could not label. He was so quiet it began to frighten me. But we just kept walking, not talking much. What I did take away from that house would fit into the trunk of a small car. Pitiful really, all waterlogged . . . but those items represented the few, still meaningful remembrances of a family that once walked this way.

It felt like Sodom and Gomorrah. Like Lot, I had been spared. There would be no turning back.

6 "Harpo's Blues"

Duluth, Minnesota, Summer, 1972

My brother Bill and I boarded a plane for Duluth, my father's hometown, where my grandmother Jen awaited us for the funerals. My eyes were glued to the sky as usual, my brother's to the ground. A mist shrouded our souls, covered up our hearts. A week and half, or so, had passed. Services and burial would be held June 17th. People set their alarm clocks. The sun came up on other days. The rubble had been cleared. The planning for a new city had already begun. People counted their blessings, went to work, made love; the clock kept ticking, and time moved on.

My eyes were still dry. I wouldn't shed a tear for thirteen years. I knew this was not normal. I even tried to cry a few times, but it was like trying to manufacture rain. My tear ducts were dry as the Sahara. Someone suggested I might see someone, a therapist? I made one appointment. We just sort of looked at each other. I have to be fair; I didn't know what either of us was supposed to say. I could have used some empathy, but it felt strange paying to get it from a stranger. My emotions were still in the deep freeze, and I couldn't thaw them out.

Answers would be nice, but nobody had those either. An explanation would help, but how could anyone explain what happened? God? I walked a tightrope between many borders. My mind wouldn't let me tip over. What were my options really? The infamous, "just let go." The pseudo-psycho advice of the time was "let it go," but something, somewhere deep inside, informed me that "letting go" was way too dangerous. I couldn't see the ground. With undefined spirituality and an as yet unclear relationship with the Divine, the prospect of blaming God for my loss didn't work either.

What if it was my fault?

There were even faint whisperings that something called "cloud seeding"—a form of manmade weather modification in which silver iodide is dropped into clouds to increase their density—had been performed in the days prior to the big event. I couldn't even go there, couldn't begin to entertain the thought or idea that the government was manipulating the natural cycles of the atmosphere.

I didn't have a place to put any of this yet, so I ignored it from stem to stern, as if it had never even happened. My family had checked out and I did, too, in a different way, into a narrow corridor. I scooped them up in my mind and moved them to the side as if they were on some kind of extended vacation. And I believe they are in a manner . . . without me.

As was my style, what I couldn't comprehend, I just filed away until further notice. Like dear Scarlet, I would think about it later. Life was waiting for me. Everyone reminded me. I reminded me. I shelved death like a new album I'd bought but lost the equipment to play. So it just sat there collecting dust, buried along with all the other music I couldn't hear. There was time. It wasn't going anywhere. All my musing could more than wait.

I did not know that my filing skills would eventually create a clutter so disastrous that no amount of vetting or rearranging would bring order to it. Until I decided to deal with the contents of that filing cabinet of grief, the heart I stored in there would remain under lock and key. I did not know how to face down the events of my past, shed the tears that would clean my heart, dress the wound and heal. I'd erected a chain-link fence around my most vital organ, and nothing could get in or out. I would be forced to examine my wounds somewhere down the road, but it was easier to pretend for as long as I could.

Intellectually, I was perfectly cognizant of the event. But emotionally, I was removed. I wasn't delusional. I knew my family was gone for good. But I had one thing on my side. Everyone else pretended that it never happened either, no one spoke of it, rarely mentioned it, and when I had permanently moved away, it was a *fait accompli*. Whenever I did speak of it, as I did when people inevitably asked about my family, I spoke in the third person. It was my story, but I was mysteriously and unemotionally involved. I never thought about the flood, never dwelled on the event. It took all of one sentence, and then after a nod or a shrug, I'd move the conversation forward.

What was I feeling? The truth is I wasn't feeling anything. Denial had a full-time post in my life. But along with numbing the more complicated emotions, denial made it impossible for me to experience love, the love that you, I, we, are all trying to give and receive in this life. No one could respond to me because nobody was home.

Well-meaning people told me repeatedly: "You survived. You are one of the lucky ones. You got a second chance. Get busy. Get on with your life." I can't tell you how many times I heard the phrase "keep busy." Translated, that means "stuff it." Shelve it . . . it's over, done. I never met anyone who had their family obliterated overnight, died, survived, and then had a clear-cut blueprint for where to go from there. By the nature and magnitude of what had happened to me, however, I would eventually be forced to examine it, to bring meaning to it.

Sometimes I wondered how holocaust survivors coped, if they had found any answers. I stumbled across *Man's Search for Meaning*, written by Viktor Frankl, a psychiatrist who had survived the death camps. He found and focused on beauty. Elie Wiesel, who won the Nobel Prize, wrote after Auschwitz, "Never shall I forget those moments which murdered my God and my soul and turned my dreams to dust." Whew.

I read Maslow, Fromm, and Krishnamurti. More reading, much insight . . . barely feeling. I was lost. They all seemed to agree it was centered on one's ability to trust in the ultimate meaning of life, self-awareness, responsibility, and finally love, the stuff of sonnets and psalms, operas, homage, heartbreak, and true healing. Marianne Williamson who lectured on *A Course in Miracles* used to say that love is the glue that holds the universe together. Well said, but if, as she also declares, "Only love is real," or in the words of John Lennon and Paul McCartney, "Love is all you need," how come I wasn't feeling it?

The love I had given and taken in spades was gone, for good I suspected. I tried to recapture it in the world around me, but it was illusive, always fleeting, a jester who fooled me. I thought about my mother's broken heart and how her aorta erupted twice, maybe for the third and final time the night of the flood. And my brother Bill's young heart, and my grandmother Jen's ancient one; hearts so full, they breached with despair. I thought about what other people did with their pain, what happened to it, where did it go. Would I, like Phoebe Snow in "Harpo's Blues," have to be a grown-up and "try to bear my life in pain"?

I didn't know how to approach it. I just saw Mount Everest staring me down, and I knew I did not have enough oxygen to reach the summit. I glimpsed a shadowless, bottomless ocean that covered the floor of the world with a shoreline that looked deceivingly like spun sugar but was in fact the finest quicksand. My eyes deceived me. It was artifice, a trick. I had no gear for either passage, but I had dreams about both scenarios.

I would be on a steep and treacherous winding mountain road with my father at the wheel, steering skillfully, climbing higher and higher, and all of a sudden the earth would rumble, the road would crack open and split the car in half, dividing us forever while each of us careened over identical cliffs but in opposite directions, falling, and disappearing into oblivion. Or I would dream that I was at Summerland Beach near Santa Barbara, running and laughing, dipping my toes into the gentle surf lapping at the edge of the water line in a clear, cloudless dawn, when a tidal wave would come out of nowhere and consume me. I left these nightmares in the morning and returned to them at night.

The other problem with the "oh-you-should-feel-lucky business" is that I didn't feel at all fortunate in the survival department. My survival came with a huge price tag, the irretrievable loss of my family. They wouldn't be continuing on this journey with me. Their train headed down the track, and they waved goodbye from the windows of the same passenger car. They were together, but my ticket was confiscated. I was, utterly abandoned, still standing on the platform.

Then there was the matter of dying. It was exhilarating. I

had glimpsed my family's destination. I liked where they were headed. It was infinitely more appealing than the trail of tears in front of me. But I knew I had agreed to be here. When I died that night and reveled briefly in the ethers on the other side, I learned that I wasn't finished yet. I'd signed a contract to stay, and I wasn't going anywhere. Earth was my backyard, and what I chose to plant in it were all my decisions. But it did leave me with an aching homesickness, a kind of longing for that beauty and unconditional love that wasn't necessarily a given here, outside of nature and the family that I'd lost.

I had a lot on my plate—a big curriculum, if you will—and I was determined to figure this whole thing out, at some point. I did alright as long as I didn't delve into the emotional stew simmering in my psyche, didn't let it boil over. That special device, denial, keeps you moving; the Pretender took care of my identity; and that mysterious click in my brain was humming fine, protecting me from myself and the consequences of God knows what beneath.

Coming to terms with the extraordinary spiritual awakening I'd experienced in death and then been forced to suppress was extremely difficult. How was I to integrate that paradise in the great beyond and make my life meaningful here with this knowledge? Such an experience was the sort of thing you kept to yourself in the 1970s and 1980s. I remember stifling a chuckle every time I heard a scientist pontificate that what I had experienced when I left my body was merely the hallucinations of a dying brain. I know without question the exact opposite is true. Our minds are just yawning, getting ready to wake up and really take us for a spin, to show us the way home. We do not die. Ask the others who've been there and back, and they will concur. No one can convince us otherwise. Things beyond our puny perceptions are vast and ineffable. I wonder that science will ever catch up, but then I am only a human being, not a scholar.

Grieving in America is done behind closed doors. We teach no lessons in grief; we abide by no rules. We have no cohesive customs. My body and soul were tied up in some kind of suspended animation where my limbs moved along, my facial expressions changed, but my heart was a hard small stone. I'd flipped that switch and aligned my automatic pilot light, just like the real pilot had in the plane that carried Bill and I to the funerals.

We were gliding through the clouds on empty airwaves. The music was gone, silenced with the onslaught of unspeakable grief. My remaining brother sat in the seat beside me. We still had each other, but we couldn't comfort one another or look into each other's eyes, not the same way Jeff and I always had. The quiet space between two people can be needed reprieve or dead weight. Our embrace was brisk and frigid as a polar wind. Our bodies were rigid, my mind anesthetized.

We were the last of the Magners, all that was left of our family, and we had the North Pole between us. Bill had just traveled halfway around the world to be with me, but he couldn't make the trip between his head and heart either. It might as well have been the Grand Canyon. I wonder if he thought it strange that we didn't fall into each other's arms and cry out. We shared blood lines, but not a touch. We had no language to communicate this new storyline.

But God, he was here; my oldest brother and a man come to take the reigns. I would follow his lead and he would make the decisions that I couldn't conceive of. Wind-chill factor aside, this wasn't Antarctica, and we sure weren't in Kansas anymore. We were on our last trip home together. There was business at hand—the matter of burying our family.

There were the coffins. William Edgar Magner, Sr., and Jeffrey Ralph Magner traveled with us below in the cargo hold. Jen had purchased a plot at the cemetery near where her husband, Ralph, was buried. There were five spaces total for my family, two at the ready for Bill and me when our time came. They are all there now, but for me and perhaps my mother. I will never be put into the ground.

I remember little of our time in Duluth other than the systematic movement of the days, my own deadened feelings, my grandmother's pinched face and weary gait, and my brother's dear presence. None of us could look each other in the eyes. If you don't make eye contact, you never have to confront what lies in front of you. Bill was methodical and even-keeled. Gram was stern, brave, and precise, keeping her armor secure like mine, just in case.

As I had seen her do throughout my youth, Gram sat at the head of the kitchen table. Now, she grunted and sighed from the pain of her wound. I can see her permanently parked there, unmovable, in the house where my father grew up on birch-lined Branch Street in Duluth. Her face disappearing into another day, tiny pink spider veins stretched across her alabaster skin. She would stare into space, a perpetual Parliament filtered ciga-rette dangling between those thick blue-veined tributaries in her gnarled fingers where, after the cigarette smoke slivered from her lips, the ashes would inevitably slip onto the white linen napkin on her lap and make landfall on the bare linoleum below. She would sit there on her throne with a bone-china cup and heavy glass ashtray for company, just like Mamba on my mother's side, sipping endless cups of weak tea, putting out smoke, and sighing in deep solitary lament like a tired queen. She was regal, barren, and bereft, her only son lost, drowned, just like her grandfather. I expected her to list like a distressed ship before fainting and capsizing altogether, but she remained as erect as a soldier ready for battle, her back arched, her eyes searching . . . for a lighthouse?

She deserves the windy description. She was an admirable lady. When her mother died young of pneumonia, Jen single-handedly raised her two younger sisters and brother. When her husband was in a serious car accident, she cared for him lovingly to the last. She was, dare I say, a true woman of substance. I looked to her then for guidance and strength in the days ahead, and now, years later, I still find myself wondering in moments of travail, "What would Jen say? What would Jen do?"

At the time, we all waited for the phone to ring. Where was Mom?

I spent time roaming through olden rooms, letting my senses find their way through the maze I was in. The house was famil-iar. It was a place I always loved, and now it provided refuge from the calamity that had erased so much of our family. I would walk into my grandfather's study and trace the spines of Ralph's books with my fingertips. I slid barefoot over the plush tapestries that covered the hardwood floors and forced the silk threads up between my toes. I sat cross-legged on the floor in front of the empty fireplace and contemplated a white marble statue of the naked Thinker who held his face in his hands, wondering if he knew the answers to the questions I asked. He looked to be in a quagmire of his own, or was it just that damn weight of the world?

I would hoist myself up onto the countertop in the pantry just off the kitchen and conjure up all the ghosts of Christmas-past dinners. I imagined setting the long elegant dining-room table, placing a leaf in the center to accommodate everyone. In my mind's eye, I draped the table with fine Irish linen, set out laven-der Limoge, rose-patterned Wedgewood, and rows of gleaming monogrammed silver. I could almost smell the turkey roasting in the oven along with wild rice. The rice was hand picked by the Indians, my grandmother always told me as she began the process of soaking and simmering it in butter and salt. Roasted walnuts on thin tin sheets sat alongside powdered-sugar-dap-pled butter cookies that cooled on perforated trays. Chunks of smelly blue-marbled cheese were laid out on wooden boards, port in fine crystal flowed, and smoke from my grandfather's cherry-wood pipe permeated it all.

Every holiday we had shared growing up lingered in the atmo-sphere of that pantry, and it comforted me. My father grew up in this house, and I felt close to him and my family when I was in it. I had no appetite, but my heart was full.

I loved my room, the small maid's room where I slept, with the sink in the corner, the lace-curtained windows facing the birch-lined street where I watched the snowflakes gather in the crevices. The mahogany-framed single bed waited for me. Long ago I had perched in the middle of the bed with a jumble of feather-down pillows plumped up behind me writing poetry that no one would ever read, daydreaming of the love that awaited me in the world, and smile inwardly, absolute in my belief that it was there in my future. I would pull the thick quilt of slippery dark-pink satin up over my head for comfort, leaving just enough space to breathe and stare into the night until sleep came along with those dreams.

This trip was different. Everything was different. The three of us made small talk and passed each other in the halls as the hours ticked towards the day of the funerals. Whatever emotions we felt remained buried in the deep freeze of that bleak tundra behind our eyes and strapped to our hearts along with all the unanswered questions. Our eyes focused forward, shallow stagnant pools staring off towards some far-away no-man's land, the sea captain's grandchild and great grandchildren searching the same lost horizon for signs of life, anywhere but here. We floundered as foundlings. Where we had once held sway to a kingdom, now our titles were lost; mother, son, daughter. Our souls were cast adrift in deep waters indeed, still hoping for rescue.

It was during this time that a kind of smaller death occurred. Aunt Millo (short for Mildred)—my mother's only sister—called my grandmother's house while we continued to make preparations for the multiple funerals. I picked up the phone in the kitchen one morning to hear her begin a tirade of questions about why we had not planned a Catholic Mass. I just stood there with the phone in my hand unable to speak.

Before I could respond, Bill, sensing my distress, pulled it away and spoke with authority into the receiver. "What? . . . Stop. Whatever it is, it's already been done. They're all gone. You aren't here." What I couldn't quite figure out was why my mother's sister wasn't there. Someone later thought Uncle Ray showed up, but nonetheless I don't recall ever hearing from those beautiful cousins ever again. And I adored them all. What happened? My father's eldest son's face turned crimson, my mother's favorite color. And with that, he put down the phone. It was over I guess. My mother's side of the family . . . poof. The air was thick with abandonment for me.

The day of the funeral arrived. My grandmother Jen, my brother Bill, and I donned black apparel, stepped into a long black limousine, and made our way to the church, the Protestant one. Mom would have loved the irony, but honestly, no one in the family would have cared where the service took place. I remember only snapshots of that day. Loads of other black town cars filled with people, bouquets of flowers, mostly red and white roses in clusters of baby's breath. And a huge white wreath on a pedestal behind three coffins that stood in a neat row.

I sat in the front row on the end next to my brother. My grandmother was on his other side. I was glued to the hard wooden pew with my narrow back burrowed into the unforgiving sharp edges, peeking over at those equally sharp-edged wooden boxes, like a timid child. I remember thinking that, at any second, Mom would walk through the door, grab me away, wrap those loving arms around me, and make us disappear from this place and time. I could feel people staring into my back thinking, "God, that poor creature . . . what will she do, what's to become of her?" I wanted to jump up and turn around and shout out to them, "We aren't supposed to be here. It's all a gigantic cosmic mistake. Leave."

I had become a disturbing piece of art, displayed in a gallery of sorrow. I envisioned Edvard Munch's painting *The Scream* in my mind. I could feel Bill's arm finally move around my bony shoulders. The minister was an alien. His mouth opened and out came . . . garble. Poor man. Who was he talking about? What did he know about my family? How could he? Had he ever laid eyes on my brother before? Had he known my father, I wondered? Did anyone here really know my family, or just "the" family? Who were these people I could hear behind me sniffling and crying. Why were they crying and I wasn't? I think in that moment my posture changed forever, my spine angled slightly forward, my shoulders curved. I became concave, concealing my chest, and protecting my heart, like a sparrow over her unhatched eggs.

I don't recall one word of the service. A reading of the Twenty-third Psalm would have been beautiful. Was there music? I don't remember hearing any music. There should have been. The kind Dad liked, not a church organ. Dad loved Sergio Mendes, that soothing South American rhythm, Bacharach's piano instrumentals, and definitely some of Satchmo's solitary trumpet. Henry Mancini's "Moon River" . . . "I'm crossing you in style" for Mom, or Judy singing, "Somewhere over the rainbow . . . birds do fly." For Jeff, Paul McCartney's "Let It Be" or George Harrison singing, "I look at you all, see the love there that's sleeping, while my guitar gently weeps."

The crowd gathered there might have been from central casting. I mean no disrespect, they were paying their respects, but it was all too much, too soon, all wrong. I was intensely private. This spectacle was so public. But if they hadn't come, I'd have demanded to know where they all were. I was also the youngest and didn't know many there. I did not want to be scrutinized or pitied. I just wanted to be invisible. I wanted to rewind the tape and go back to the day before that dreadful night and change the ending.

There was a long drive to the cemetery for the burial. A procession stretched out behind us with a string of long black hearses leading the way. A stream of headlights strung together in a caravan. It was a summer day, but I was cold, from the inside out. I would stay cold for the rest of my life. When we arrived, there were three huge holes in the ground, perfectly spaced next to one another, one for each box. I couldn't watch my family going deep into the earth. They belonged above it, alive . . . not below, dead. When the lowering began, I sought refuge in the back seat of my grandmother's navy Chrysler and stared out the window in the other direction. I refused to be party to this macabre charade.

Afterward, some people came to Jen's house for food. There was drinking. I tried a half glass of red port, my mother's favorite. It tasted bitter, so I sipped just enough to honor her. Bill had another beer, and Jen, heavy-duty scotch malt. It was grim, a grim fairy tale. People ate finger food from trays and walked aimlessly around the house. I sat down in my grandfather's chair with my arms folded in front of me, my lips tight, and nodded. After awhile I went upstairs and hid under that big pink satin down puff, retreating into my childhood, waiting for everyone to leave.

I don't remember how long we stayed in Minnesota. Bill had to make his way back overseas to complete his tour of duty. He was headed for Guam. I felt like I had let him down, not being able to bridge that gulf between us. He would get back on a plane and fly far away, never to return to live in the United States. He had effectively escaped, except for one thing. Bill carried my mother's broken heart inside his chest.

I don't remember finding my way back to South Dakota. But this I do remember. I belonged with my grandmother. I should have been with her, stayed with her. But I didn't. I left her, abandoned her. I let her down, too. We left her all alone, like we had just flown in for another family summer vacation, only this time the family was not coming back. The family was dead and buried, silenced, beyond our reach. My heart had hardened, but I still felt shame.

Jen lived long and strong, but after the tragedy, she was never the same. She barely let anyone come near her, and she stayed on in her big empty house alone, refusing any help. She continued to drive the old-fashioned, oversized navy-blue Chrysler with the funny fins to and from the store. By this time in her mid-eighties, she fell from her bed one night and she languished on the floor for days with a broken hip until her little sister Helen came round knocking. Unable to reach Jen by phone, Helen sensed that something had gone awry. She found her there on the floor in terrible pain, semi-conscious. She called an ambulance. Gangrene had set in, and Jen's leg was amputated from the knee down. For her, it was all but over, not from the festering physical wound or what a once-proud woman considered her humiliating condition, but from the injury we had no antidote for . . . the organ that got our family every time . . . her damaged heart.

It's a given that no parent is supposed to outlive his or her child; you hear it again and again. It's unnatural. Jen had no spares. She might as well have been on that crumbling rooftop that took my father, or scrap it all, the prow of that ship at sea. The sea captain's granddaughter's heart was beyond repair, waterlogged, and soaking wet up to her soggy red-rimmed eyes. It was time to close them and join her son. The bagpipes of Scotland were calling her home. I faced this truth when I flew into Duluth to see her the last time.

I gently picked up her hand to say, "Oh, Gram, I am so very sorry." And she answered back, "Norma, is that you, dear? Is Bill here, too?"

Forgive us our trespasses. . . . Forgive me.

7 Quicksilver

I flew back to the Black Hills after my family's funerals. I took everyone's advice. I filed it. I got on with it. Forget about picking up what remained of the shards of my life, I intended to rebuild it before the mud on the ground was dry. Someone recently handed me a small program for a memorial service for my family that was held locally at the Campbell-Paula Funeral Home on Thursday evening, July 20th, that summer, but I have absolutely no memory of it whatsoever. Strange days. In many ways, I lived in the world of W. H. Auden's "Funeral Blues." The clocks had been stopped; the wood had been swept; and the stars had been put out.

I rented a furnished cabin on Canyon Lake. It was a simple one-room cottage with knotty pine walls, a slightly vaulted ceiling, and an over-sized picture window that ushered in the western light. I reverently placed the odd remnants from my parent's house. On a shelf, I propped a lone black-and-white photograph from the early 50s, an impromptu portrait of my family taken at Lake Saginaw or Mackinac Island where we summered as kids in Michigan. On the coffee table, I placed my father's heavy glass ashtray, the one emblazoned with sports-car insignias. On the bureau, a Christian Dior perfume bottle—Diorissimo—that once stood in my mother's medicine cabinet, and on a top shelf, safe and high, I slid an unfinished oil painting Jeff had been working on. It was a rendering of the structure, strangely enough, that had saved my life. There was so little left of the precious cargo from the lives of three near and dear to me, things that they had touched, held, used, and imprinted. Besides the memories, it was all that was left to me.

Out of the jet-blue sky, my high-school partner in crime, Catherine Bachman, arrived from California. She was a true beauty who'd transferred to Rapid City our junior year and sent minor shockwaves through the halls. No one had seen anything like her. By virtue of the fact that she was from somewhere other than our small town made her an exotic. She was striking. All she had to do was smile and the guys would trip over themselves, unable to string two words together. Her parents were divorced. She had been living with her mother in Los Angeles but had come to stay with her father in South Dakota. After graduation she went back to the West Coast to pursue an acting career. She was single-minded and focused. What she "may" have lacked in talent then, she more than made up for in confidence and ambition. I admired this in her. She always knew who she was, exactly what she wanted, and she would go on to get it.

I, on the other hand, was a kind of lost gypsy, incessantly restless; absorbing what surrounded me and then moving on, constantly in motion, never letting too much grass grow under my feet. Like my maternal great-grandfather H. O. Anderson, who had prospected briefly for gold in the earth's veins, I was on a digging expedition of my own. But my search was not for anything tangible. My pursuits were spiritual in nature. I was on an ambiguous quest. While others were concerned with careers and starting families, I wrestled with my inner demons, traipsed over international datelines, and tripped over myself and God while I missed the hidden, priceless gold that coursed through my own bloodstream.

I had been with Catherine in Los Angeles prior to coming back to Rapid City that fateful summer. And now into my little cabin she came to bunk in with me, to check on me, and probably to make sure I hadn't lost my mind or something more. She realized it was not a time for me to be left alone to my own devices, and she was a self-possessed young woman of action. Catherine was always a bit ahead of the pack.

Immediately, she insisted that we go to the site in the canyon. It was actually the last place I wanted to be, but others seemed to find it irresistible and compelling. As I said, it was our ground zero. It was an empty stage. The production had closed; the props and furniture were all but obliterated; and the characters had packed up and gone. The theatre was dark. My armor of denial was settling, beginning to fit rather nicely.

We jumped into my mother's conservative gold-and-white Dodge sedan, making our way past the fish hatchery, Cleghorn Canyon, and up the highway towards what remained of my former life. I wasn't necessarily resistant to the idea. I wasn't looking for anything, nor had I any expectations from this little excursion, but there was, for others, an inexplicable curiosity attached to the site. It was just another trip up the canyon to me.

The house was fairly gutted at this point. I would guess the watermark was about five and a half feet high inside. As we walked around outside in the thick brown muck, surveying the aftermath, I looked up at the sky, my focal point, while Cathy looked down. We were in the front yard. Suddenly Cathy let out a sound. "No way, . . . look what I found," she shrieked. My heart skipped a beat. Found what? I walked over to where she had bent down in the semi-dried earth. She had spit on something in her hand and was rubbing the dirt off on her shirt like she was polishing a stone. She was. It was my mother's diamond wedding ring, which she didn't wear often. She wore a simple gold band. This was a later, larger model that Dad bought her on one of their anniversaries. She kept it tucked away and wore it only on special occasions.

Soon others were standing around eyeballing my mother's ring. Sure enough, one of them, a so-called friend, grabbed it up to admire. Then, he slipped it into his back pocket. An awkward silence followed, until my best-friend Pam Radtke's sister, Cheryl, said, "Hey, where did that ring go?" The guy's face flushed, and he looked away sheepishly. It was not a tasteless prank. Again, thievery reared its ever-prominent, ulcerated head right under my nose. This bastard intended to make off with the last vestige of what was left there in the dirt.

It couldn't have stunned me more if he had cut it off my mother's finger right in front of me. At last he pulled it out of his jeans and held it up in the air. I didn't have the awareness to realize I was witnessing the workings of criminal minds there on the periphery of my own circle. My mind didn't comprehend blatant deception from the outside. Things would happen directly in front of me, personal items would disappear and reappear in front of my eyes, along with people, and it simply didn't register or compute. I didn't see it or learn from it.

A bull's-eye was etched on my forehead for the entire world to see. No wonder I felt transparent. The look on my friends' faces when that ring came out of the rubble spoke volumes about my cluelessness. I didn't even reach for it. Had my mother walked up to me then, I might have believed in God again. This ring was a lovely thing to behold, but honestly, I could have torched the whole lot then and there. The shell of what was once my home was treated like the town dump, a free for all.

These excavations bruised me. Catherine's heart was in the right place, she was trying to help me salvage something there from that awful night, and I am grateful. My other dear friends were there to hold me up, metaphorically speaking, but what about the others, picking things up there in that desolation? They were violating me, my family, and the place itself. Whatever else that remained there in the dust and the dirt should remain. We were standing on sacred ground.

I was beginning to learn that security does not lie within the material things of this world. True security is an inside job. But this instance was just the first of more to come in the sleight-of-hand brand of temporal illusion that I wasn't prepared for. It would become clear to me that life was not about the accumulation of anything, but my white flag of surrender wasn't even dangling at half-mast yet. (The ring languished in a metal box for years. Weird. I never wore it and hardly ever took it out to gaze at it or touch it, although it was a perfect fit. I no longer own it. I'll be traveling light when I leave.)

Anyway, for now, denial was the only thing between me and the men in the white coats. I was still holding my breath just above the water line. If I wasn't at Horse Thief, Pactola, or Sylvan Lake—back on the water, swimming and water skiing—I was sunning and camping in those glorious Black Hills with friends. I escaped into all that was familiar and that I knew I could do, what came naturally. Meditation, reflection, introspection? They were not allowed. I just wanted to go on living and grab onto my former identity quickly, without missing a note, a heartbeat. So I ran, tumbling headlong into my hereafter.

I'll never forget the night I had left home the first time, at seventeen. My mother wouldn't speak to me; turned her back on me. I thought she was angry. I didn't realize at the time that she was merely sad. Her baby was leaving the nest, and she couldn't stop me. A rite of passage was taking place. We hadn't known that in less than two years our separation would be irretrievably complete. A Lakota holy man once said: "What is it the white man wants? They are never content with what is, but always wanting more. What is it?" Good question.

I was a dreamer, weaving wanderer's dreams. My wings were tightly tucked beneath my shoulders for the time being, but it wouldn't be long before I would ruffle them open, spread them wide enough to fly away to the golden West Coast, where I knew my destiny waited for me. But for now that reality would have to wait . . . just a little longer. I was too restless for my own good, always ready to feed the wanderlust, engineering the next adventure, planning my great escape. I couldn't exhale. There was too much life in front of me.

God and I weren't on speaking terms yet. I have to admit that made me a bit nervous, but not enough to slow down. Did I even believe in God? I don't know what I believed, but I could taste, touch, and smell life, if not the totality of my own feelings. My mother's words echoed in my ears, "Life is short, don't waste it." She also said something else that I filed away, "Live in peace . . . because. . . ." But the rest was lost, like me, and floated away behind me.

Quicksilver: Mercury, the planet closet to the sun. I was combustible.

8 Higher Ground

In my little rented cabin on the lake, I was still smack dab in the center of the flood plain, just a few miles east and a short hike from my former home. I felt safe, I guess. I was perfectly present, perfectly calm, perfectly separated, mentally and emotionally, from the tragedy that had enveloped me. My heart had closed its doors and wouldn't reopen for decades. The event that had ripped my family apart overnight and nearly taken my own life turned me into a textbook shell-shocked soldier, a walking-wounded "private" without a uniform. I had no plan of action other than the matters at hand. What I did possess was this peculiar lack of awareness that served as my protection, so I was bulletproof; yeah, right.

HUD (Housing and Urban Development) brought in trailers for those who had been left homeless by the flood. They were available for the moving in. I qualified, and a two bedroom, one bath had my name on it. It sat up on a flattened, grassless hilltop on the north edge of town, another landscape I'd never seen before. It was barren and sterile, all these white tin boxes on wheels, cloistered into rigid rows, perched up there on the prairie. I was grateful to HUD for the housing. I thought it was astounding that a new home was provided for me. Somebody cared. Somebody was watching, even if it was big brother. I wrote a letter to President Nixon to thank him.

While I was unpacking new dishes from Kmart during my first week in the sleek new aluminum shoebox furnished to me by the federal government, I plunged my hand into a cardboard box to pull out a thin drinking glass and cut the base of my right thumb almost to the bone. Thankfully I was not alone. One of my quick-thinking friends fashioned a tourniquet from a dish towel to stop the bleeding, and we rushed to the local hospital, where they stitched up my hand. It left a perfect, heart-shaped scar.

My second trip to the hospital that same summer was more serious. I was coming back into town on Sheridan Lake Road from a roundabout trek to Spearfish Canyon with Bobby Weber, a good friend. He had a shoulder-length mane of brown hair with a full beard and mustache, huge brown eyes, and a sweet disposition. He looked a lot like George Harrison. My brother Jeff had sported the same look. He was in the driver's seat of his yellow Volkswagen with me alongside. My new Saint Bernard pup Alice (after Arlo Guthrie's song about the restaurant where you could get anything you want) was up on my lap. It wasn't even late, maybe around 9:30 P.M. We hadn't imbibed, although we might have been smoking a little grass earlier in the day. Not unusual. We were returning from a true joy ride, enjoying ourselves.

It had been one of those seamlessly mild and pleasant summer afternoons like countless others in the Black Hills. As we came around the wide bend near Arrowhead Country Club on the outskirts of town, a car appeared on the horizon. Its headlights were on high beam, blinding us. It got closer way too fast, on our side of the road, in our lane. All at once, we could hear the sound of a carload of wasted teenagers hollering and hanging out the windows, weaving wildly all over the road, but coming dead on for us. There wasn't time to react. Before we knew what hit us, I was hurtling into the windshield at over fifty miles per hour and headlong into a world of hurt.

My head exploded as I was thrown from the car and landed on the harsh asphalt shoulder. I don't know how long I was out, but when I did come to, I immediately tried to get up to look for my pup. When I opened my eyes, I thought I was blind until I realized it was blood flowing into them and everywhere. Miraculously, Alice was thrown clear onto the soft, grass-cushioned meadow nearby. She was whimpering, but fine. Bob was unscathed as well.

A nurse, coming up from behind, saw the whole thing unfold and stopped in time to push me to the ground and keep me stable until the ambulance arrived. I passed out again and don't remember that ride. I was in the hospital for days. My head was split open from the bridge of my nose to the top of my cranium. I suffered a concussion, and it took numerous stitches to close the wound. I recall little from my hospital stay except lying on those bleached sheets, realizing that I'd skated past death's door once again. Now I had three scars. Two were visible on my face and hand. The deeper psychological wound was unseen, but festering, just below the surface.

This close encounter with heavy machinery would be my third before I was out of my teens. I had totaled my brother Jeff's vw bug late one night, escaping injury altogether, and another time I ran a stop sign and crashed my own Corvair convertible. I was thrown clean away onto that unforgiving asphalt again. My father, on his way home from work, found me lying there in the middle of the road unconscious. I only mention these incidents to punctuate the serendipity operating in my life, karma, whatever you want to call it. I don't believe in luck or happenstance. When it's your time, you will be called home and not a nanosecond before. It doesn't give anyone a license to be reckless, or a pass . . . only pause.

I like to think my mother must have been aware. I'm sure she was there watching over me, probably shaking her head. Maybe she caught my pup in midair and gently laid her on the ground nearby. She had to have known I was walking an uneven fine line here.

9 Deadwood Daze

My friend Alecia, Rhonda Buell's older sister, moved into the trailer with me. We were both working, having lives. Somehow we started to play canasta, and we got so hooked that we would squeeze in a hand or two before, after, and between work. We never played for stakes, but we kept score. It was fun. The summer was coming to a close, and we planned a trip somewhere. She was thinking about becoming a professional card dealer and wanted to learn 21, blackjack, and work in the casinos. We decided to go up to Lake Tahoe to check it out. It was beautiful up there, uncharted territory for us both.

When we returned a week later, the first thing I saw was my front door, wide open, flapping and banging away on its hinges. My new stereo system and television were gone. My new home was stripped bare. But this time, it was Man, not Nature, that had stolen all I had. The stuff of my life was disappearing on me again. I suspected that it wasn't a random robbery but the work of a couple of the pitiful lowlife punks who had conspired to rip off other personal belongings in front of me. I bumped into them from time to time, and they always smiled and hugged me like we were good old pals. Too creepy, but alas, I could never prove their guilt or innocence, so they remain nameless.

A small army of us spent those long Dakota winters on the slopes of Terry Peak, skiing and partying into the wee hours on the weekends. Each season, I bought a single-piece stretch jumpsuit—green or black with a matching down jacket and vest. I braided my hair, loaded up the eight-track stereo in the Saab with my favorite tunes, and roared up Interstate 90, trekking to the mountains to spend the day, singing all the way, tapping out the beat on the dashboard. The winters were cold. The temperature was in the single digits or dipped off the thermometer altogether some days, but nothing stopped us from piling into a car and going for it. More than once the wind-chill factor was at least forty below zero. No big deal.

We would usually stash a bottle of wine in the trees and periodically dodge off the trail and head into the pines for a toke and a sip. On any given day, a group of guys from the Mountain Goat Ski Shop would be there, or a handful from Deadwood, Lead, Spearfish College (Black Hills State), or some of my brother's old friends. And if I drove up alone, I was confident I wouldn't be for long. People teased me if they spotted me on the way. The music blared along with me mouthing the words to some song.

We'd all rendezvous around lunchtime, make a quick pit stop, and adjust our bindings; stack our skis upright in the snow where we stood, like toothpicks on a big white cake. We'd chow down, laugh red-faced with abandon, then race right back up the hill for more, insatiable.

Inevitably someone would be available to meet at the famous Number 10 Saloon in Deadwood at the end of the day. The Number 10 was a big beautiful saloon with high ceilings and history to spare. It boasted a long, high, dark-oak, polished bar with sawdust on the floor and plenty of room in the back for pool tables and live local bands. The table where Wild Bill Hickok played his last "dead-man's hand" at poker and was shot in the back by Jack McCall was still there, along with the chair.

We'd trudge in, fresh from the slopes, damp from the snow, bone-tired from the exertion, but brimming with tales of a close encounter with a tree, an unexpected bump, or a collision with the chair lift or a friend. We reveled in all the near misses, our eyes widening in the telling, our confidence soaring. We'd throw down a Jack Daniels, or a hot buttered rum, maybe a shot of tequila to take the chill off. I remember a time or two it was so cold that the locks on our car doors froze solid, and we laughed and pulled out a Bic lighter to melt the ice. I still marvel at how we drove those pigtail roads during blizzards in the midst of blowing snow and black ice after leaving the bar late at night. It is a minor miracle to me to this day, but I don't remember a more carefree, exhilarating, and wonder-filled time. We always made it home safe to ski another day.

The freedom of being strapped onto those narrow waxed boards, flying down the mountain, turning and bumping along on carved moguls with the wind in your face and hair, navigating the terrain with your own pure skill was nothing short of magic. These were some of the best days of my life. We were invincible, in love with our lives, so fearless.

One night, while I was home in the trailer, the wind started blowing hard, and before I knew what was happening, I found myself trapped, alone on that barren little hill in a box, caught in a bona-fide blizzard. The trailer's thin tin walls buckled and heaved so wildly I expected them to collapse. I imagined the snow bursting through the walls, burying me, and wondered if someone would find me before it was too late. I thought about George Mallory lost high in the sky on Everest in white-out blowing snow and wind. I wasn't comparing myself to him in climbing skills or fearlessness, but I was forever interested in stories of survival, especially those that involved the unforgiving elements of Mother Nature. Been there, done that.

The pilot light on the furnace kept going out, and it was getting colder. I sprawled on my stomach on the floor repeatedly, turning the gas lever with one hand and lighting a match with the other. It would ignite, but immediately blow out. That Bic was of no use to me now. I heard the wind in its frenzy and felt my fingers numbing. The electricity faltered, too, and then it went dark for good. Oh, man. Finally I gave up, took a flashlight, and burrowed myself into a closet. I wrapped blankets all around me for protection, shuddering while my heart pounded. The Fates were toying with me. I took it as a sign. It was time to pack it in and leave.

I went back to Canyon Lake, ground zero. I moved into a larger cabin with my girlfriend Vickie Plummer. The cabin had a massive natural stone fireplace where we burned endless cords of wood around the clock in the winter. It was our main source of heat in those long northern months. Night and day we kept those logs burning.

Then a real fire erupted one night in the cabin behind us. We smelled the smoke and saw the flames jumping about. We rushed into the darkness in our bathrobes. Vic pounded on the doors and windows to wake the occupants. She managed to get them out in the nick of time. They were profoundly grateful and wanted to thank us with a home-cooked Indian dinner. They went to a lot of trouble to prepare the meal. When it came to the party, I was a no show. I don't know why I couldn't go. It was impossibly rude and out of character for me, and it bothered me enormously.

Maybe all the near-death and dying stuff was just too much for me. It was Vic who had saved them, anyway. She was the hero. I was just there. I sent her along with my apologies and some excuse. Why couldn't I save anybody? Why couldn't I rectify the way things went down the night of the flood? Why had I lived and Jeff died? Unanswerable questions tormented me.

At the same time, another bank of storm clouds gathered overhead. Late one night, Vickie's brother Ed was killed in a freak car accident. He was Jeff's age and hung out at the cabin with us. She was devastated. They were extremely close. She and Ed shared a bond as strong as the one I shared with Jeff. We had both lost our beloved brothers now.

Although I was still numb, living in that non-feeling place where nothing serious could get in, Vic and I spoke of our brothers at length in front of the fire that winter with dark red wine sliding down our throats, mingling with the memories. We draped our arms around each other and assured ourselves that, one day, we would find them together, soaring through the universe, free at last. Could they see us now, feel our love, change a thing? We knew they were sharing musical realms we couldn't hear.

My mother was right. Life is short, and the only constant is change. Was Nietzsche right? Did the good die young? I kept looking over my shoulder. Something was pressing at my back. No, it was my stomach. I was pregnant.

There was no decision to make. It was a clinical condition that I could look at methodically and unemotionally. I did not ask questions, I did not search my soul. . . . I just got in my Saab and drove to Denver for what they euphemistically called a D&C. Then I got back in my car and drove straight back to the cabin in the Hills. I was in excruciating (yes, I deserved it and more) physical pain. Within the week, the clinic called and said that the pathology tests had come back from the lab and that they didn't get it all. What did that mean? I was still pregnant. Unimaginable. I got back into my car and drove all the way back to Denver and repeated the whole process all over again. I was humbled.

I never told the child's father. But I have never forgotten. I never forgot the child I didn't keep, the soul I chose not to bring into this world. Giving birth to a child is something I would never do. And I am not being glib. My heart was simply closed, not even under construction.

There was movement afoot, however. Now my back was arching, my shoulders ached. I couldn't catch my breath. I was already gone.

10 "Long May You Run"

It was time to go. I would leave for the coast alone this time. I was ready to roll, but first, there was a rock-and-roll rendezvous and someone I was supposed to meet. It better be quick. I intended to leave the next morning at first light. That evening, Pablo Cruise, a hot new band from northern California, was exploding onto the local scene. They wore vintage Hawaiian shirts and sang about how it was "all right once you get past the pain," and later, "when my baby smiles at me, I go to Rio."

My friends and I wore low-slung hiphugger denim cutoffs, flimsy cotton Indian-print pastel shirts. We adorned ourselves with silver and turquoise and donned huge dark glasses. Our bodies were bronzed from basking in the afternoon sun at the lake, our waist-length hair naturally streaked and loose. We were, as Neil Young once wrote, "twenty four and . . . much more." We were invited backstage. Out of the corner of my eye, I could see a slender silhouette, the tallest man I'd ever laid eyes on, six feet four inches with a devilish smile, long straight blonde strands of hair falling over his forehead and around his ears. He winked as he walked past me.

I have learned the hard way that you do not find or seek love. It will find you. The heart has a Morse code, and that code is your destiny, even if it is not a fairytale ending. Those that you are supposed to meet will be in your path, and you don't have to do anything to make it happen. So the man in front of me knew me, and I him. We just hadn't recognized each other yet.

I can't say it was a traditional relationship. This was rock and roll, after all. I did not cling to him. I knew there were others, and I wasn't moving to Marin County, but we meant something to each other. I adored him. His face was both masculine, with a chiseled square jaw line, and boyish, with a mischievous grin and an inviting playfulness to his gait. The surface glamour of the music business appealed to me. The music—it had been instilled in me by my father and my brothers.

His name was Chuck, and as part of the road crew, he had a lifestyle that many men envied. He lived in a candy store and was able to sample a bit of it all. He never pulled his hand away, saying, "Ah, no thank you, I just want the one with the white chocolate center." Life was an all-you-can-eat smorgasbord. The combination of wine, women, and song is an intoxicating mixture. Who could blame any attractive young man in his prime, the world at his feet? And this was the 70s, early 80s. No one had even heard of AIDS.

I was heady with freedom, too, and when the concert ended, so did my time in Rapid City. I left South Dakota in my rearview mirror and headed straight for Malibu, where I quickly wore out my welcome with my newlywed friends, Catherine and her husband. I stayed in their guesthouse overlooking the Pacific Ocean. I was high on my new life and youth, irresponsible and irrepressible, while those behind the scenes collaborated on a television pilot that would "make" Catherine's career and catapult her into our living rooms for years to come. She was to become a prime-time icon in short-shorts, a character named Daisy.

It was a short jaunt up PCH (Pacific Coast Highway) to the most alluring little coastal village I had ever seen. I fell in love at first sight, and I knew that Montecito is where I would unpack my bags. Splendid Spanish-Mediterranean architecture saturated the atmosphere, more reminiscent of an elegant movie set than a place you could put your feet up and live. And pristine beaches from Miramar to El Capitan, famous for surfing, dotted the coastline. Heaven.

I rented a three-bedroom bungalow off Coast Village Road near Butterfly Beach, and it was here in this contemporary paradise that I met and worked with two important women in my life. German-bred Heidi Becker was a contradiction, her loveliness belying the determination and strength not apparent on the surface. I would trim her long straight hair on my porch in the sun and point out strands of aquamarine, seashell pink, and pearl white. It gleamed like abalone. I would tell her, "I think you've come out of the sea, Fräulein, a beached mermaid." She loved the water and sun, all it touched, and it caressed her in kind like Botticelli's Venus. She tooled around the village on a little Vespa, her hair streaming behind her in the warm breezes, a colorful pastel skirt wound up in a knot around her knees.

Lovely Leigh, another Libra and kindred spirit, I met while the new restaurant at the harbor on Stearns Wharf was being built and getting ready to open. She was to be the staff manager and hired me on the spot. Leigh possessed boundless energy and was so smart that I would sometimes have to ask her to define words that she used in conversation. The day I met her, she wore a red cotton T-shirt with the Lee jeans logo emblazoned across her ample breasts. How fitting. She was Gidget, wholesome, fresh-faced, and freckled, always upbeat, near the beach with a "beach boy" trailing after her, and I thought she was the epitome of cool . . . she was . . . and is. She worked three jobs to raise two kids and still had time for everyone. She managed her time and other people well and all with an even hand, those scales of balance. I later talked her into moving to Los Angeles because I thought her intelligence begged a bigger venue.

I dated, but not seriously. My boyfriend at the time, Russell Fox, and I were driving around another quaint little community just south of Montecito called Summerland, where we happened upon an empty two-story Cape Cod house overlooking the ocean. It was like Martha's Vineyard West, built into a hillside on almost an acre of land with avocado and jacaranda trees, a greenhouse, and even a terraced little vineyard. I paid next to nothing for it and made it my own.

And then, another great love came into my life . . . a golden retriever pup named Mr. Wheatie (Russell's idea, a good one). Everybody called him Bugsy. I called him Monk. He answered happily to whatever and whomever called him and grew into ninety pounds of unconditional love. When I returned from work, he always waited at the end of the driveway, with either my tennis shoes or a pair of tennis balls in his mouth, tail wagging, and ready to go directly to the beach. Oh, joy.

He was my trusted, beloved, steadfast companion. The hours spent frolicking with that dog represented something we both coveted and believed in—freedom. And we shared it for four years. One day he ran ahead to hold a more everlasting space for me. I've kept his ashes in an urn on my kitchen shelf. I thought I would scatter them on the beach he loved, but I can't seem to let them go. "Long may you run," Monk, . . . long may you run. Those were the best years of my life, right up there with skiing.

During the holidays, my kitchen was a center of activity, packed with people who had no family and no place else to go. We'd light the stone fireplace outside on the patio and open up the house. Every available chair was moved outdoors to accommodate friends from all over the country. At my home, friends became my family. I nurtured those relationships like the pure gold I knew they were. We cooked together, drank good wine from the valley, and shared our stories, losing time until the ashes died out and the sky lit the dawn. Engaged in life to the fullest, we barely noticed the passage of time. Life was not a tragedy. It was a revolving door filled to capacity with activity.

A breathtaking woman named Carol Hayes arrived one day for a visit with a man named Kyle whom I used to ski with at Terry Peak, and she ended up staying. She was a talented artist who painted landscapes and my house in pale pastels of moody blue and gray watercolor shades taken from the sea until the time came for her to move on.

One evening James, an old friend from the Bay area, called asking if I might help a mutual friend who was moving to Santa Barbara get her feet on the ground while setting up a brand-name hair-products distributorship called Paul Mitchell. "Fine . . . give her my number," I said. In no time flat, a tornado made landfall on my doorstep. Cecilia was a dynamo. I had no idea what I was doing, but I tried my best over the next few years, making sure that all the better salons stocked her products on their shelves. She had done a lot of rock-and-roll hair in San Francisco back in the day, so I had a live-in personal hair stylist for a while. She made me blonde for the first time, and I stayed that way for a decade. I'm blonde now, just to cover the gray.

One evening after an aerobics class, we were hungry and wasted no time. All sweaty with no makeup on and with my hair done up in the usual ponytail, we decided to stop at our favorite sushi bar on State Street. While we sat at one end of the long countertop, Cyl started flirting with two young men at the other end. I was tired and barely noticed. Cyl liked to flirt, and she was good at it. The guys eventually moved in closer, and the tall, dark-haired one came over and sat down next to me. Before I knew it, I had given him my phone number.

He called straight away. We dated only briefly, lightning speed. He was ready to take it to the next level for his own reasons. He ran a seafood restaurant near Stearns Wharf and was about to be transferred, first to northern California and then still farther north to Seattle, to franchise and open additional restaurants in quick succession. Things escalated at warp speed.

I was still seeing Chuck in Marin County sporadically. I made a phone call and planned a rendezvous with him, jumped on a plane, and flew north to San Francisco. We shared a flawless, fine weekend, as always, but this time, at the conclusion, I asked the sixty-four-thousand-dollar question. I leaned in, made direct eye contact, and ventured, "You don't really want to be in a relationship do you?" It was straightforward and clear-cut, requiring a yes or no answer.

He cocked his head to the side slightly, as if he didn't hear me correctly, and paused, caught off guard. I repeated it. With his eyes focused over my shoulder, he said rather tentatively, but definitely, "No." I had my answer, albeit soft spoken. That was good enough for me. I held Chuck's face between my hands and kissed him on the forehead. Waving goodbye, I boarded my flight back to Santa Barbara.

I started planning a wedding in my head almost immediately. I was thirty-one and woke up one morning realizing I wanted to get married. I never had the feeling that my biological clock was clanging in my ear and I needed to have a baby . . . yesterday. But by then, my friends were taking the plunge, and it seemed like the time to partner up.

My handsome restaurateur proposed. In three weeks, we put together an elegant wedding at the El Encanto Hotel on California's Riviera with seventy of our closest friends. The outdoor setting in the gardens was exquisite. I wore an ivory wool suit and hat with a subtle veil that just covered my eyes. Cary, my intended, was beautifully turned out as usual. I do not recall who gave me away. Was it his brother Steven? Monk wore a red bow tie around that thick yellow fur neck. Stunning. My dearest friends cried when I wasn't able to. I have a photograph of them, all beauties, each and every one, lined up in profile, all in tears.

Women cry at weddings. But I didn't. I was unable to squeeze out a single drop on what is supposed to be the happiest day of one's life. But I was efficient. I packed up my house, my life, and Mr. Wheatie, my Monk. I was bound for points north, my favorite direction, to start a brand-new life with a brand-new husband. The day was December 30, 1983.

11 Rain and Ragged Dreams

Seattle, 1984

It was pouring rain. It always was. Cary and I had found a nice three-bedroom on a friendly street in the suburb of Kirkland near the new restaurant. His days and nights there were long. The restaurant was his wife. Mr. Wheatie, dear Monk, was my son. Once I started working and taking classes at the local college, Monk was left to sit in the rain by himself. We walked together, but there were long hours now when Cary and I weren't home, and this fact weighed on me. Monk and I were used to being together every day, strolling in the sunshine, body surfing on Summerland beach, following our noses. The textures of our turf had changed. We were both confused. We both felt alone and far from the home we had created in Summerland.

Cary and I were alike in many ways, both physically and psychologically. We were slender and energetic, sensitive, cerebral and inquisitive. The only glitch was that we both married on the rebound and too quickly. And it was never meant to be. We barely knew each other. Our courtship was abbreviated; our union premature. Monk and I were both miserable, and I suspected Cary was as well. I thought that our marriage meant that now everything would naturally and automatically fall into place and become the way it had been when I was growing up. I'd gotten a pass and I was safe. Everything would be okay now. Being married meant I had a family.

It was in Seattle that all the loss and trauma I had suppressed and stored since the flood began to seep out as surely and as relentlessly as the Pacific Northwest rain. And my body began betraying me in a long slow dance of fear and panic. I was back on a rooftop needing rescue. I began to experience a series of physical symptoms—aftershocks, if you will—that shook me to my shattered little core. It was as if I could see myself from the outside in, but I had no access, no key that fit. I was there, watching another fissure widen, but I didn't have the grout to seal it back up. I was locked out of my own house, and yet I was trapped within it, unable to get out. I was buried alive, inside myself.

Out of the deep blue, in the rain, away from my beloved home, I began to shake. Little tremors at first, nothing radical, but along with it came heart palpitations. When it overtook me, I thought my heart would pound right out of my chest. I couldn't catch my breath. I initially thought I was having a heart attack, but as quickly as it came, it was over. Then without warning it happened again . . . and again. I became a captive of irrational terror.

I confided in Cary. He was baffled and blown away. I could see the disbelief registering on his face. Where had his fun wife gone? He didn't sign on for this. What had he gotten himself into . . . a dreadful mistake? Was he stuck with flawed merchandise? He looked at me and said, "Fix it. Get some help." He was right. It was a job for a professional. I proceeded to find one, or so I thought.

I sat in a cold office before a woman whose walls hung with degrees.

"Why are you here?" she said from that tunnel far, far away.

I started to talk. I gave her some background and mentioned the flood, my marriage, the move, my irrational panic. Between long pauses, I described my symptoms. It was excruciating. I searched the outline of her face for some sign, some assurance, some empathy, some answer, a click, something, anything, but it wasn't forthcoming.

Our fifty minutes were up. She wrote a prescription and pushed it toward me without meeting my eyes. I don't think she said anything else to me. She just stared out the window. She seemed depressed. In my hand, I held a prescription for lithium. I knew the professional was dead wrong about me, about this. Lithium was a drug for patients with bipolar disorder, and that was not my problem. Intuitively I just knew it; something deep in the core of my being told me to turn tail and run.

Now, I have the highest respect for the therapeutic model, but I believed she barely understood me, possibly had tuned out entirely, and I wasn't so shut down that I was cut off from some basic human feeling. I certainly felt no compassion coming my way. She never bothered to ask me a single relevant question, and here she was eye to eye with a young woman who had lost her family, nearly her own life, and, damn, she never even asked me about it? Too weird. All I knew for sure is that she was the wrong doctor . . . for me. Hell, maybe there were no doctors for whatever ailed me. Oh, dear, now what?

My past had caught up with me. I was about to enter a frontier. I desperately began my own research, scouring the college library where I was taking classes. I read Elisabeth Kübler-Ross's *On Death and Dying.* I found a book called *The Courage to Grieve,* by Judy Tatelbaum. But there was little information to be found. The page I needed, the one that said: "You've been traumatized. Everything you're feeling is normal for what you've experienced. You're not going crazy," did not exist, had not been written yet.

I did discover the work of two scientists, Kenneth Ring who wrote a book entitled *Heading toward Omega,* and Raymond Moody who wrote one called *Life after Life.* Both were doing groundbreaking studies on near-death experiences. I was beginning to remember mine. I attempted to connect the dots. If I could find understanding, then I could, as Cary so aptly stated, "fix it."

Studies on war veterans and the effects battle had upon them and the brain were just beginning. They called it PTSS and PTSD, Post-Traumatic Stress Syndrome/Disorder. I hadn't survived the battlefield and man-to-man combat, but I had lived through a traumatic tangle with Nature and its aftermath. The symptoms are similar, if not identical in some cases. It changes you in ways you can neither predict nor fathom.

I realized what I'd been experiencing were full-blown panic attacks. Panic places you in a state of hyper-vigilance. You feel that you must be ready to respond, to react, maybe even to save your own life. You remain in a perpetual state of heightened awareness, certain that the worst is about to happen. And I wondered if the "worse thing" that could happen could be the fact that I had survived the flood. I know, that sounds crazy.

I read something helpful years later. Another lay person who was coping with its devastating and lifelong effects explained it this way: "Many people don't understand PTSS. It's not just emotional, it's physical, it messes with your brain synapses and ability to regulate mood and sleep. You repetitively experience the intense fear of the moment you thought you were going to die. No one can really empathize. Survival becomes painful. Everyday you question your purpose in life and its meaning." Gawd. Saving my own life was about to become a full-time job.

I continued to search for someone else to help me. I called around until something clicked. Just when I was beginning to lose hope, a gentle man on the other end of the phone listened to me describe my symptoms, then said, "I think you just need a safe place to feel the feelings." It was music to my ears, elixir for my soul. There were layers and layers of myself to unravel and weave back together again, and I didn't know how to do it. Was it possible he did? When this man looked at me, he didn't look afraid, afraid like others did. What a relief. Someone was there to walk beside me through this. I'll never forget Cary's first response when I told him my panic attacks were related to the flood. "Aren't you over this yet?" *Merde*. I had barely begun.

I began having precognitive dreams. I think they started about the time I began to get in touch with what they called my near-death experience. I called it dying. This "knowing" was something I brought back with me, a side effect of being on the other side, if you will. I was "touched" in a way. Was this a good thing? I would dream things and they would happen, or I would know or intuit things in a most acute way. I had a dream one night that Cary and I were in his convertible with the top down, driving south along Pacific Coast Highway near Carmel where we'd spent our honeymoon. We went around a steep dangerous curve in the road, catapulted over the cliff, and crashed onto the rocks below. When I came to in the dream, he was nowhere in sight. I woke up in a cold sweat. I knew it was over. That we wouldn't be traveling down any more roads of life together. My marriage wasn't even on life support.

It was around this same time that I did have a prophetic dream. In this one, I saw palm trees, clear blue sky, and a two-story building off in the distance. There was a staircase that looked like a stairway to heaven. I was drawn to it as if in a trance and began to climb. An elderly couple was standing at the top. They were archetypical Wise Ones, a perfectly complemented pair. They nodded as if they were expecting me and opened the door. I stepped into the room, and it was filled with books, lining every wall, stacked on the floor in every nook and cranny. There was a large white bed in the middle and a window with westerly light. Palms lined the landscape as far as one could see. They didn't need to tell me it was California. I knew that state would be my new home. I just didn't know when the proverbial "shoe would drop."

I started to find American Express bills for flowers I hadn't received. The phone bill had long-distance numbers I didn't recognize. My husband came home later and later. As I said, my intuition was acute, and I sensed there hadn't been any real closure where his former girlfriend was concerned. I suspected they were in communication. I was right, and they would reconcile once I had "checked out" for good. We all have our reasons for the hasty decisions we make. It astounds me how naïve we can be when it comes to the really big and important ones, believing our happiness can be found in situations that only compound and bring to the light our deepest fears and unknown selves. I knew I was responsible, that I had driven another loved one away. So would begin a pattern where all I loved would disappear.

I imagined my mother's disappointment, my father's concern; the cocoon my family would have wrapped around me, simply loving me. I should have had the presence of mind to call my brother, book the first flight to Bangkok, and run headlong into his arms. I still had family at this point. Bill was far away, but he was still on the planet. The thought never crossed my mind. We were both still residing on foreign soil so far from one another and ourselves, that the distance was immeasurable. He would have opened the door wide and let me in to stay for as long as I needed. God, I needed him. Whatever kept me from him, I deeply regret to this day.

A call came from Cathy. She came through the wires with an opinion and the guts I lacked. "Get out of there and come to LA." Best advice she ever gave me, and she was a woman with a lot of advice. The house I still owned in Summerland was not a consideration. I didn't like going backwards, and besides, the house was full of someone else's life. LA wasn't my first choice, but it was my only choice. It was close and I had friends there. My grief, this homework, could wait a little longer. Get back on the wheel as fast as you can, wasn't that always the solution?

How many more times could I deep-six it and make it all stay down? The panic had subsided enough for me to function, but I was still in trouble. I wasn't different from anyone else out there in the world, but my secrets separated me from them. Even the professionals were in uncharted territory.

12 Mirage

Los Angeles, 1985

Thomas Wolfe said, "You can't go home again." I knew it was futile, folly, but I did the next best thing. When I got to Los Angeles, I went to live with my mother's oldest and dearest friend. They had known each other when I wasn't even "a twinkle in my father's eye," and she came to my rescue. She had a beautiful two-bedroom apartment in Beverly Hills and offered me sanctuary. I felt like shattered glass, like my outline was marred with hairline fractures and my warranty had expired. She opened her home and, more importantly, her heart to me. I was grateful to have a mother's influence.

Betty Couglin is simply lovely with a teenager's giggle but also a deep wisdom I savored. We shared cups of tea like my grandmother and I had, me entreating her for advice and, of course, stories about my mother and father that only she could know. She and her husband and my parents had both been young couples in love, who had supported each other through the births of their children and the flourishing of careers and lives on the same track. I liked Betty's neighborhood, a quiet enclave situated just down the block from the Peninsula Hotel and behind the Friar's Club. She had a big extended family with grown sons who had known and loved my brothers. Betty spun for me a gossamer safety net, wrapping me in the warm cocoon of family for restoration.

I didn't want to wear out my welcome, so as soon as I could muster up the strength I began to search for an apartment. I got in the car to check out the neighborhood, to hunt for signs of people on the move and places that had not yet been advertised. That was how I had found my house in Summerland. I put up my antenna. I believe you can choose where you want to be and it will find you.

I drove across the street past Beverly Hills High School and Roxbury Park to a small street called Shirley Place, originally named for Shirley Temple. Half way up the block, sure enough I spotted a sign that was just going up. I climbed the brick steps all the way to the top, to the very back and, "lo and behold," there was the exact place I had dreamed about—the white-washed brick façade, the staircase, the room exactly as I had seen it in my mind, now before me in living color, every detail. I knew it was supposed to be mine.

There was one small problem, actually a ninety pound problem. It was too small for Monk and also too dangerous. Olympic Boulevard, which is adjacent to Century City, Beverly Hills High School, and Roxbury Park, was a crowded and popular thoroughfare. But this was temporary after all. I called some friends, two of the best people I knew, in San Luis Obispo, JT and Sue Haas. They also went back to my carefree days on the ski slopes, and we remained close. JT was originally from Bozeman, Montana, where Sue landed for awhile in college. They met, fell in love, and eventually moved to the West Coast to follow opportunity and grow a family . . . wonderful, down-to-earth people whom I trusted implicitly. They offered to board Monk on their "ranchette" just north of Santa Barbara in Atascadero, ideal for grownups, kids, animals, big gardens, and indulging a love for horses.

I had visiting privileges and drove up on the odd weekend. It was bittersweet. When I left, Sue told me that Monk would slink off into the garage for days and not come out. He felt abandoned, too. He had been there for me, and now I had dumped him and gone. Every time I drove up, he probably thought I was there to retrieve him and that we would then pick up where we left off, be together again. A chink in my denial armor took another hit. His love was hard to ignore and be without. My heart didn't trust the love of human beings, but this teddy bear in a fur coat soothed my soul. He reminded me I was loved unconditionally. But I left him.

I made haste, turned the page, and set up another new life.

Things moved so fast. By this time my grandmother Jen had passed. A trust fund she created for me provided income, and additional funds came from the rental of my house in Summerland. The panic attacks subsided enough for me to feel that I was ready to figure things out. I wanted to study art history, humanities, and literature. The surface I had skimmed in psychology never went deep enough. I was thirty-four and had been running for well over ten years. I knew the answers I sought lay within my own undiscovered, disowned self, but I still needed the books, and some travel suited my need for speed, that insatiable urge to keep moving at all costs.

Of course, the consensus was that I should begin dating right away. But it was going to take a lot more than a tall dark stranger to fix what was wrong with me. Knowing that, I projected, "You will never get close, don't even try." Devastating to admit out loud. No one had a chance and neither did I. My friends were just doing what came naturally, setting me up. They wanted to see me smile again, to bring back the old carefree Merlyn.

She was long gone by this time. The music in my head had begun to fade, along with the faint shimmer of light behind my eyes. I couldn't find her anywhere. I didn't trust life fully. It had blindsided me. I looked over my shoulder for an ominous sign. Movement meant safety to me, always that forward motion propelled me on.

My first date was with an "industry agent," Jack Gilardi, who had been married to a child star, Annette Funicello. I don't know where this one came from. He was amiable, kind . . . it was alright, but going nowhere. He said something to me on our second date like, "Look, I know we're not in love, but it would be nice to have someone attractive on my arm at these events I go to." I accepted his flattering compliment, but it was not enough to make me agree. Relationships were something I couldn't fake. If it wasn't lightning, I wasn't feeling it. I was not that girl, not a great dater for the sake of it.

Even so, it was through one of these dates that I met one of my dearest friends, a lanky model named Ellen Fuchs. She was disarming and unpretentious. She never grasped her great internal beauty, carefully masked behind the external. And her deadpan wit was spot on. She, like me, was skilled at keeping love at bay and would freely admit it. "Why can't I take the good medicine that will make me feel better?" she would say. "Why do I prefer bad medicine? It always makes me sick." Ah, the dilemma of the perfectly fine female forever entranced by the superficial glamour of the bad-boy persona. We became fast friends.

My new neighbor, David Mirsky, was a writer and like a big brother to me. He was anxious to hook me up with a man he knew, someone he thought would be perfect for me—perfect except for the fact that he forgot to tell me that Wayne had only been separated from his wife for two weeks. But I was too wounded to notice. We both were. And besides, we were going to meet sooner or later anyway.

The first night he came up my stairs and into my life, I knew him from a waking dream I'd had while I was married. When I opened my door, I immediately recognized his voice, his accent, and the first words out of his mouth. It was déjà vu, a glimpse of precognition, confirmation that our paths would indeed cross, and here he was. We had our first dinner date, and he flew off to Paris the next day. He worked for a major studio, Warner Brothers, in the worldwide end of things and travel was built into his job description. He was sophisticated and worldly and smelled of expensive cologne and sweet cigars. We were equally matched in our dating experience at this point in time, I think, but sadly our hearts were both closed.

Here was a man, not a boy. He reminded me of my father; the beautiful way he dressed, his manners, even his face, the cut of his jaw, strong features, his height, well over six feet, and his broad shoulders. He drove a Jaguar. The interior even smelled familiar. An older couple once stopped us leaving a restaurant and remarked how beautiful we were together. We never fought or treated each other with anything but tenderness, but something was missing—a part of each of us. The fraction remaining wasn't enough to build on, and at some point, I knew the match would be a fractured fairy tale. And it was. In my experience, men usually leave it up to the women to figure out it's a bust. The women have to call them out and clean up the mess, while the men can disappear neatly, without a trace. Then our natures leave us to figure out why we weren't the one.

He and I went back and forth for four years until I pulled the plug. I'd been waiting for him to get over his divorce, and he was just waiting; waiting for his wife to come back to him, maybe, I wasn't sure. He would say, "You know I love you." I couldn't feel it? How could I have? I wrote him a letter telling him that I felt like I'd stayed at the party too long and wanted to leave with some of my dignity intact. I knew if I didn't make a move, we could drift for years. He told me to hang in there; the relationship would "evolve." Was I impatient? I was lost, but still rational enough to know I was compromising myself each time I saw him.

I began to think, as my friend Ellen had so poignantly said to me at one point, "Well, he's relationship proof." She was referring to him, but she was describing me. I've never been desperate with regards to my own security. I never expected it to come from a man. The thought never crossed my mind. I had my own money. I had always been alone; I had never really let anyone in; so how could I miss what I never had? I was good to go. I was a one-woman professional moving company. Problem was I was running out of storage space. I just kept stacking it up and closing the door. The warehouse was getting full. My failed relationships were piling up, and I was shutting down.

I had the will and the means to keep running, and so that is what I did. I became the artful dodger, the organizer of things that didn't matter, blinders firmly in place. Damn, that denial was doing a fine job. It was then that I began to travel in earnest, to circumnavigate the globe, immerse myself in other cultures, other landscapes, and foreign soil. My wandering took on new dimensions, epic proportions. If a ticket to Saturn had been possible, I would have stood in line for one.

I went to work for Cathy. She was good to me. She was making appearances all over the map on behalf of the success of her new show as well as her new-found status as a bona-fide celebrity. She asked me to tag along as her traveling companion, and I even managed a television credit for hair and makeup on a few occasions; all in direct measure to her generosity and clout with the network and my good fortune. I am grateful to this day for the extraordinary adventures we shared. For two young women off to see the world first class, . . . well, for the most part, we had a blast.

We went to the Amazon in Venezuela, where we bathed in the pure, tannin-based ice-tea-colored waters at the base of Angel Falls. We camped in the heart of the rainforest, where orchids grew in abundance like dandelions, the size of rubber plants at the base of the trees. We canoed along isolated stretches of the Amazon; there weren't other human beings for miles. We had to helicopter in with supplies, all we would need for the special called *World's Greatest Stunts:* Catherine and I, along with a cook and the best stunt artists in the world. Bicycling off the magnificent falls and camping under the Pleiades, I wondered at the beauty and magic before me. This was it. This was a smattering of what I had glimpsed from the other side . . . a sliver of godliness right here on earth.

Then we were off to Russia, the Soviet Union, to film a "lifestyle special" for another network. It was during *perestroika*, restructuring, and *glasnost*, the opening. We were in the middle of history in the making. We traveled from Moscow to what was then Leningrad and down to the Baltic along the Black Sea. Arriving there was like going from Technicolor to black and white. We were struck by how little the Russian women had. No cosmetics, no decent undergarments, no tissues or tampons, none of the simple luxuries we took for granted. It was an eye opener. We left behind most of our own stuff, giving it to our female guide and interpreter, Ingrid, to keep and distribute to her friends and family. And later I would send care packages over, wondering if they ever got past customs, aware of the corruption and need everywhere.

We felt like spoiled relations and privileged to be there, to be treated so graciously, generously. We drove by people lining up on the streets for a few bananas. Estée Lauder was hosting a grand opening nearby. I wondered who would be able to buy anything in that expensive cosmetic "line." What a dichotomy. Our hotel looked tired and leftover from another century, which

I rather liked. The carpets were threadbare; the corridors wide and filled with intrigue. The heating system was old as well, and I was constantly cold. We had to swat hungry cockroaches from the sink when we brushed our teeth. An equally threadbare wire held the light fixture that dangled from the ceiling. Another world within a world.

Cathy looked at me at one point and said something like, "This may be too much for us, Mern." I had no reply. Our pampered, Western sensibilities were rearing their culture-shocked heads. But . . . there was the other side also, the history. We went to Anton Chekhov's house, where he had written *Three Sisters,* and we filmed a walk-through at the summer palace of Catherine the Great. It was golden, literally dripping in it. We were humbled at Yalta, where Stalin, Churchill, and Roosevelt signed the peace agreement at a secret summit during World War II. I was overwhelmed by these glimpses into the past, and then . . . at the end of three weeks in the Soviet Union, we were ready to return to the West.

When we arrived at Heathrow in London, we were whisked away to the Saint James Club and two spacious suites. The concierge brought us hot tea and scones and arranged for excellent seats to *Miss Saigon* that very night. It was a complete departure, an about-face from our time in Russia. We took no time for reentry and departed almost immediately for the theatre, where we were seated front and center, staring up from the footlights in our finery. I remember taking in the opulence of it all, the contrasts of our experiences, and feeling quite odd.

The curtain rose and a helicopter landed on the stage! The music came up and a loud crescendo peaked during the second act of the production. Cath and I looked over at each other and started to tremble. We reached for each other's hands, squeezing them together while tears streamed down our cheeks. In that moment there was no separation between us. There were no words. And it wasn't the play. I will never forget it. I think we slept in the same bed that night. We had been through something . . . two worlds had converged and collided . . . divergent and extreme. It would take some time to integrate and reconcile them.

It was Christmas in London. The streets were awash in primary colors and light. There was a real sense of wonder in the air. We decided to walk out for some retail therapy. We set off for Harrods and Harvey Nichols. We bought warm cashmere and found Molton Brown, the apothecary where they made hand-milled soaps and hair brushes. And then it was time to go back to America.

My restlessness wouldn't leave me. London at Christmas began a pattern for me. I would always travel during the holidays. Get on a plane and make sure I was in some removed, unfamiliar hotel sipping a champagne cocktail or having high tea so that I wouldn't have to think about the family that wasn't there and remember that I was alone. And it was a way for me to weave new memories in cities from Dublin to Delhi. So that's exactly what I did for over twenty years. I had a syllabus if you will . . . a list to complete.

When we returned to the States I went back to work for Cathy, but my heart wasn't in it anymore. More loss was catching up to me. It was during this time frame, the following spring of 1991, that I penned the farewell note to Wayne, quit work, and decided to run away to Bali. I craved the majesty of nature. I did this time and again. When things oppressed me, began to weigh on me, I felt the need to be surrounded by and drenched in natural beauty. I wanted to be in a land far, far away where no bad thing could seep in and where I could listen to and feel in sync with the rhythms of the natural world. It was always hard to make travel agents understand that my intention wasn't to be sitting on a crowded beach somewhere in front of a high-rise hotel, looking to "hookup."

No, I wanted to be high on a cliff above a rain forest in a place I'd never heard of, in my own private Shangri-La. I took a seventeen-hour flight to Denpasar, drove to Ubud, and checked into a cliff-side room with a balcony hanging out over the rain forest exactly the way I'd imagined in my vision, and here I was. This place actually existed, and I'd found it, up in the trees and farther away than I'd ever been. On a cloud.

I sat and wrote in my journal or took long walks through the village, wondering if the sight of Hindu temples would inspire me to pray. I was about halfway through my stay in Bali when I awoke one morning in pain. My lower back hurt, and I was going to the bathroom constantly. I thought it was probably a kidney infection. The driver at the hotel took me to a local doctor, who was located in a small hut filled with children and mothers who were also in some kind of distress. I described my symptoms, and he prescribed the proper meds for a bladder infection.

The pain didn't go away, but increased. I was doubled over now and couldn't walk. I thought I was going to pass out. I was worried. I called the desk, and this time the driver took me to the local hospital. They gave me a shot, and I slept for almost two days. When I woke up, the driver, a beautiful young teenage boy, had gone and come back. He brought me some of my things from the hotel, sat with me, and interpreted for me with the doctors. He hand fed me from trays of hospital food and helped me with a sponge bath.

There was never a glimmer of impropriety. When I went for x-rays by ambulance, he was there next to me holding my hand. Lying there on a cold steel examination table, I saw geckos the size of small cars running across the ceiling overhead, and the young man was glued to my side. We took short walks on the hospital grounds and ventured farther out. We shared the natural beauty of his homeland and talked about his large extended family, such a contrast to mine. I never mentioned my history. I only wanted to hear about his life, his little nieces and nephews, all his brothers and sisters, his parents, aunts and uncles.

I didn't know how to repay his kindness to me, although it was never expected. I did give him money, but he gave me more. He gave me back a piece of the puzzle that fit, and I believed. He was pure goodness incarnate. Stuck in that hospital bed so far from all that was familiar to me, I knew that home was as near as my own heartbeat, this room. God was everywhere, especially Bali, behind the innocent eyes of a stranger, in the guise of a caring boy. He eased my worn soul, showed me what peace might feel like, and reminded me who I was. He turned my heart inside out, and I was alright. I was going to be okay.

13 Black Monday and *The Big Chill*

In the late 1980s, something else happened that seemed like a mere blip on my screen, but it registered a nine on my financial portfolio. It was October 19, 1987, and would come to be called Black Monday. The London Stock Exchange broke all records. Never had so much money been lost so quickly by so many. I was on that list.

I called Jay, my accountant, and he said that I probably lost close to sixty thousand dollars that afternoon, but not to worry, it was cyclical, would always come back. It wasn't the whole thing. "Be patient, don't worry." I would wait for it to come back around. It was just some numbers on a piece of paper that I didn't have in my hand. And I trusted him in these matters. I was still getting monthly checks and didn't realize until much later that they were being cut from the principal instead of the interest. I had never intended to touch the core of that fund. I didn't want to "know" about it, but I benefited from the interest that it generated. I was never frivolous or speculative, but respectful. If I let it sit there, I figured at some future point in time I would know what to do with it. That day never came.

When it started to shrink and eventually evaporate, a "friend" not so delicately commented: "Well, it's not like it was really your money. You didn't earn it." I looked at her at that moment and thought about the pound of flesh I'd sold to the devil in exchange for that money. I could have taken another pound from her, if I'd had the strength. She would be pleased to know when the final day of reckoning came, I would say out loud verbatim, "I made that money go away." Restitution/Paid in Full. It was blood money, and I knew better than anyone that it was never mine. I knew that it would extract a bill from me at the end of the day. I knew that all it had done for me was to allow me a chance to stare into the looking glass.

My family was not here to look out for me and guide me. I was on my own without benefit of their council, at the mercy of strangers. I didn't see the eyes of the scavengers in the trenches with me. Like teenagers in all those freak car accidents, I never saw it coming. Homes disappeared. Cars were stolen; things went missing in the night, got permanently lost in my world. My money, your money, all money comes and goes, as all temporal things of this world will. It's just money. But it forced me to look long and hard at the way it makes us behave. And losing it brought another kind of grief, one in which I lamented letting my family down by letting it all slip through my fingers.

Those who managed my money put a higher value on it than I had. For them, money bought fine things. I never saw the sumptuous offices just across the street in Century City that I paid for along with those Armani suits, shared the charming banter as they secured others' futures and holdings while mine went up in smoke. I was a Savings & Loan and didn't know it.

For me, money was a meager replacement for a much greater loss. How does one measure what another's life is worth . . . what love is worth? What is the going rate for a family these days anyway? What would it take to put mine back in the room? A few million dollars, some blue-chip stocks, cash in some life insurance, the American Dream? It would never be enough to bring them back, to glue the pieces of a shattered family back together again, to replace the love, to stop the rain.

Over the next few years, I would lose it all, everything. By this time I had liquidated my stock portfolio and invested in commercial real estate, apartment and office buildings, including the profit on the sale of my house. It all went south in the worst real estate decline on record. I wasn't a business woman. I never understood how a fine family fortune could be systematically gutted and rendered worthless, all in what was just another day in the life of business. Was I naïve? Had I trusted in error? Probably. I put everything but my heart out there for the taking. Let the money handlers do what they do best. Look after it; keep it safe for me. Let it grow, they told me. Oh well, . . . the only real estate I had was the expensive space I was renting to my old pal denial. It was solid enough under my feet for the moment.

I returned to college and worked odd jobs. I had a little savings. I traveled to Italy with a group of art buffs from UCLA to see Michelangelo's *David* and Raphael's Madonnas. I went to the Vatican to buy some rosary beads and see if I remembered my Our Fathers and Hail Marys. I wondered if God was looking or listening. I wondered just what I believed.

Then I made my way to Greece and danced on white rooftops as far as the eye could see. I inwardly laughed hearing my mother sing Peggy Lee's, "If that's all there is my friends, then let's keep dancing. . . ." The credo of the examined life as prescribed by the ancient Greeks is "Know thyself." For many, I guess it's just another credit you need to matriculate into the next classroom. The one I was in was keeping track of my absences, and apparently I was a slow learner.

In the dead of winter, I ventured off to Scotland, my ancestral home, to see what I could feel. I drove to Balmoral where I stayed in an eighteenth-century castle nearby. The view from my beautifully appointed room was breathtaking. I closed my eyes and breathed deeply. I was back in my grandmother Jen's house in Duluth, or she was here in this room with me. I bundled up and walked to the small cemetery across the road and scanned the tombstones for names and dates. I wasn't necessarily looking for my own; I was in my motherland, wafting across the moors into the past. I had slipped through time once more. I soaked my traveling bones in a white porcelain tub with claws identical to the one on Branch Street and ordered pots of strong Scottish tea. I expected the wallpaper to start talking to me. I missed my family.

When I left the country, reality set in. I was detained at the airport. When they inquired why I was traveling in Scotland, a routine question, I told them, "I am a writer." It was the first time those words ever slipped from my lips. Why? I'm not entirely sure. I was embarrassed to say that I was a student because I knew I looked too old. Certainly, I had been keeping a detailed journal at the time and recording every nuance of my visit hoping for clues to my identity, but I wasn't making a living as a writer. I think it was a latent, romantic notion. It wouldn't be the first time I stepped off the side of the world and into my own creative plotline.

Those next few holidays, I spent in London and Paris respectively. En route to Paris I met a woman wrapped up in a big brown fur coat in the check-in line who was reading a book. We gravitated to one another and struck up a conversation, discovering that we shared more than a flight plan in common. We were staying in the same small hotel on Rue St. Honore near Place Vendome.

Rocchina was a statuesque Italian who was just as interested in art history as I was. We hired a car and driver and filled our time at the Louvre, the Musée d'Orsay, the Picasso and Rodin museums, and drove to Versailles. I think I combed the museums of the world to see if those who deemed it impossible to duplicate natural beauty, futile to try even, were right. But I also appreciated the fact that we attempt to reproduce such beauty in art. I have great respect for artists, and I spent much time wanting to see if we had succeeded, in my humblest of opinions. Churches and museums were my sanctuary.

I dipped my fingertips in Holy Water and knelt to light candles for my family at Notre Dame and Ste. Madeleine cathedrals, a ritual I would repeat in every foreign church I could find. I scattered my prayers with light and rosary beads, a throwback to my Catholic upbringing. I had the most peculiar feeling the entire time in Paris that I can only describe as more déjà vu. As I walked along the Seine at dusk, I felt a pervasive melancholia that was irrational. I started dreaming in color.

Rocchina had family in Eze, a coastal village in the south of France just west of Monaco. Her aunt and uncle invited us there and tucked us into the terraced apartment above theirs. It overlooked that picturesque coastline that so reminded me of Santa Barbara. Each day brought drawn-out, home-cooked five-course meals, along with vintage wine and stimulating conversation that lasted late and long into the evening. They treated me like a daughter. We could hear the hum of the cars from the Grand Prix roaring by periodically just around the bend, but we stayed away. The film festival in Cannes was going on then, too, but that circus didn't interest us either. We weren't looking for crowds or distraction. We both felt reflective and solitary on this trip. Once we'd ridden the rails along the coastline, it was enough to be right where we were, peacefully overlooking it, wine glass in hand, and day-dreaming, free.

I continued to ratchet up the frequent-flier miles, collect my stories, and try not to forget my sense of humor or the faces of those in front of me. It was during this time that I solidified more close friendships. There was a small group of us from South Dakota who hung and played together, and we all simultaneously wound up on the West Coast. There was Cathy, the actress; Carol Hayes, the artist and Ford model who later moved to New York; Tamara Taylor, a Susan Sarandon look alike who won awards for producing the news at a major network, and me. My dear friend Pam (Radtke, then, Lester now) would visit periodically, but she stayed behind in the Midwest to raise a beautiful family. Kay Ann Lux, also drop-dead gorgeous, dropped in occasionally when she wasn't flying to Southeast Asia for Northwest Orient, an airline. I was the runt of the litter. They were all attractive and accomplished, and when I was with them, I felt like the wild flower in a bouquet of long-stemmed roses.

There was a New York contingency, too. JoAnne Curtis worked in public relations at CBS, the same network that aired Catherine's television series. JoAnne was originally from Saint Louis but made New York her town from the moment she set foot there, married a writer, started a successful career, and also raised her daughter, Emily. She was savvy and so full of fun. She escorted us around the Big Apple when we all first met for a television event there, the annual dropping of the ball at midnight in Times Square on New Year's Eve. It was one of those moments in time when you look back and realize there were other forces at work, drawing a group of people together. Those were good years.

Last but not least, there was Clifford Campion, originally from the West Coast, Orange County. He made his mark as a screenwriter, came "out" in the 1980s in New York City. We all cherished and adored him. He lived in New York for many years, but he eventually migrated back west to Los Angeles when the AIDS scare became too real. He moved into silent-screen star Clara Bow's nostalgic old apartment off Sunset Boulevard.

Together, we went to art openings and screenings and fabulous parties on both coasts. We had a bit of faerie dust in our pockets and didn't know it at the time. Cliff bought a home in Palm Springs, too, where we hung out, sunning, swimming, laughing, and sipping cocktails underneath the stars. He used to say "his girls" reminded him of the group from the film *The Big Chill*. Aside from JoAnne in New York, "the girls" were all close friends, kids who had grown up together in the Dakotas, gone on to bigger lives in the big city, doing interesting things. I was the vagabond, stuck on cruise control, floating through lives.

While our story didn't contain a suicide as in the movie, we suffered a great loss when Cliffy contracted AIDS. At the time, little was known about its potentially devastating ramifications. All we knew was that fear was rampant, and we all were trying to get up to speed with information, but so little was available. For me, Cliff was a surrogate brother—as good as it got as far as having someone in your corner. He had old-world class, impeccable taste, that old black magic, real panache. He was a natural storyteller, and we gathered around his feet like children. He wore this sort of beat-up floor-length beaver coat all over New York and let me wear it all over Europe in the winters. I reached into the pocket once and pulled out a matchbox from Air Force One and giggled with delight. He was always full of surprises and fun. Sometimes we'd sit on his floor, drink martinis, listen to Rachmaninov concertos, and converse seriously.

He was also a Christian Scientist, and when he got sick, without medication there wasn't much time. We all rushed to his bedside. At first I wasn't sure if he knew me when I bent over his bedside to kiss him good-bye for the last time, but when I looked closer, I was certain he recognized my touch and grinned his Clifford grin. I thought he was traveling between worlds about then. He didn't linger long. He danced away quickly, taking the music he loved with him, leaving the rest of us in silence.

He died on the 23rd of December, right before his birthday, but he took his final bow the next night. I was at the Bel Air

Hotel sitting in front of the fireplace on Christmas Eve when I glanced over my friend's shoulder and, nonchalantly as you please, said, "Oh look, there's Cliffy . . . he just winked at me." He wore his favorite red bow tie (a sweet reminder of Mr. Wheatie at my wedding), a sharp black tuxedo, and raised a crystal glass in my direction. He looked happy, peaceful, and incandescent. Impeccable.

As soon as the words came out of my mouth, I knew it was impossible. I blinked, trying to get him back in my field of vision, but it was too late. He had vanished . . . slipped through the thin sheath encasing him and into the ethers . . . just beyond reach and out of time. Christmas would always be bittersweet.

14 Dark Continent

In the early 1990s, another spectacular adventure came my way. This time Catherine was doing a pilot on location in South Africa for a television series called *African Skies*. She invited me and Pam, who was still living in South Dakota, to come. Pam had married and given birth to two sons and a daughter, bright and fine human beings. But she traveled to the West Coast frequently, and we planned some great trips together later on when her kids were grown.

This 1990s trip would be a reunion of sorts. All we had to do was get there. Catherine enticed us with visions of a house, home-cooked meals, the promise of safari. We couldn't pack our bags and get there fast enough.

Catherine was there to meet us in Johannesburg, but when we pulled up to a high-rise hotel, Pam and I were both confused. Not only was there no house, but there was "no room at the inn." It was inconceivable to me that we had come halfway around the world to find that we did not even have a room to sleep in. Instead, we were whisked off to a film set in a remote location. But we were in Africa. If we were going to see it, we would have to make it happen. Pam's sister Sandra had a friend in Zambia, Iqbal, who owned a small private game reserve. We found a travel agent at the hotel and made arrangements to leave as soon as possible. We were dying to experience a true safari.

We got a flight northbound to Lusaka and were met by Iqbal's friends. They took us to his compound in Ndola that was surrounded by barbed wire and armed guards. It was eerie passing through those barren gates in the dead of night to enter a gray cinder-block house, see guns mounted on walls and strange men drinking dark whiskey. We weren't sure what we had gotten ourselves into. After a restless night, we made our way onto a private air field at first light and found ourselves boarding a former "Flying Doctors" plane, an old relic that was used for charter. As we got into our seats, the belts were broken, and when we looked down, you could see right through the floor to the treetops below. I quickly made the sign of the cross, and we bowed our heads silently. The Our Father and Hail Mary were on our lips in unison. The engines were too noisy for talk, and it was one of those "hand grabbing" moments again. When the pilot reached for a beer, we surrendered big time. Neither Pam nor I will ever forget it, and we laugh out loud, wide-eyed with wonder still, in recollection.

Once we landed and settled in, my breath caught as we watched the light gradually change and play off the most stunning sunset I'd ever seen, layered in rich rare pastels. This remote terrain was so still, the beauty raw and immediate. We were alright. I let out a sigh and looked over at Pam. She was content as well. We'd arrived . . . and it was good. After dinner and thick mugs of black coffee, we set out on night safari.

The jeep was a double-decker, open affair. The night had darkened to pitch, the moon hidden from view. Just when I wondered how we would see anything, the jeep lurched to a stop. "Look down over the side," our guide said, and he shone a bright light right below us. A pack of hyenas huddled within feet of us. When they bared their fangs, I thought they were the most ferocious creatures I'd ever laid eyes upon. My heart pounded. They were so close.

As we continued along what was left of the riverbed, we came upon a sad and pathetic sight. There in the middle of the bed was an impala stuck up to her neck in mud. It would be a matter of time before hyenas would move in for the kill. Pam and I were shaken by this development. "We have to do something to save it," we cried. Our guide shrugged his shoulders and repeated the age-old adage: "It's the survival of the fittest. The weak die young. It's the rule of the wild."

We had other ideas and insisted that we stop to release this poor animal from certain death. For some reason, the guide indulged us, and every able-bodied person got out. We formed a circle around the impala, digging until she was loose enough to pull free. I started to tear up. I wanted to reach out, stroke her forehead, soothe her, and tell her it would be okay. Her eyes were wide, black with fear. The poor thing was exhausted from the struggle. The men picked her up and laid her just beneath my seat on the lower level of the jeep. They closed the gate, and we drove away.

About a half hour later, there was a loud thump under my bum that startled me. The driver pulled over and said, "She's probably gotten her legs back." The impala had regained her strength and was trying to get up. Then, the most incredible thing happened. Her whole body began to shake. She shuddered from head to hoof. The spasm ran like fallen dominos from the tip of her head to her legs. She glanced at us quickly, paused for the briefest moment, and then bounded off into the night.

I thought about how clean this release of energy was. I found this utterly fascinating. Nature had a way of taking care of near-death trauma in an efficient and expeditious way. For these animals in the wild, it was absolutely second nature; built in. I wondered what made human beings different? Why couldn't we throw off terror and threats to our safety in this simple natural way? Why did we civilized beings get stuck, the energy trapped in our bodies, ever tightening, battened down like a ship in constant, permanent distress. Why couldn't we move through it, adjust, and move on as in nature? Why couldn't I? Big "wow" for me.

That night in our little huts, we had just gotten to sleep when we thought we heard thunder, which of course it wasn't. A herd of elephants came straight through our camp so close you could feel the warmth of their breath and their hides skimming the sides of our flimsy walls. Elephants fascinate me. Studies have shown that they live in a constant state of chronic post-traumatic stress, always being hunted, always on the move now.

We spent a little less than a week in the camp, then headed straight for Zimbabwe to see the grandeur of Victoria Falls. We went to the Livingstone Museum and looked at all David Livingstone's artifacts and correspondence. We sailed down the Zambezi River, watching brown-backed hippos rise and float along in silence until their large shiny eyes finally blinked. They stared straight at us, the rest of their mammoth bodies submerged, like subtle submarines. We saw rare black rhinos, more wild elephants, zebras, and giraffes.

After a week in Zambia, we were ready to head back to South Africa and see where the trail led next. We flew south via Lusaka, anxious to get to the Cape of Good Hope. On the flight, there was a male attendant who appeared to be almost seven feet tall, probably from the northern Masai tribe. He had the most sensitive eyes and gentle demeanor I had ever encountered in a human being. We spoke briefly and said nothing of consequence, but he brought water to my eyes.

This has happened to me only three times in my life, when I have beheld a stranger and instantly been impacted in a way I had not expected nor could explain. The other time it was an usher at a theater in Westwood many years ago. He must have been seventy years old and either didn't need the job or really did and it was his livelihood. He seemed so out of place in the commotion of a twenty-something college crowd, no one paying him any notice. But there he was, individually greeting each person with a quiet dignity, tearing their tickets in half, and sweetly smiling. All I can say is when he looked at me, I felt my eyes welling up again. Both of these men, continents apart, exuded a kindness, a gentleness I cannot describe, but could only feel. The third time it happened, it would be the Chief of the Fulnio tribe from the northern Amazon in Brazil. When he looked into my eyes, I felt completely transparent. My heart opened and turned inside out. He barely spoke English, but he looked so deeply behind my eyes I knew he could see all my secrets. One glimpse and you are moved, taken in. He said, "I know you. I understand you." Whew.

Soon we were off to Cape Town to tour some of the finer vineyards and keep a date with another wild animal. We wanted to drive along the coast toward the Indian Ocean. We were in a minivan with a few other passengers and a guide, when we spotted a family of baboons along the side of the road. They were hungry and foraging for food. Before you could say "lunch," we pulled over and slid open the side door to take some photos. Suddenly, one of the male baboons swung into the van. He was dead set on seeing what we had in our plastic souvenir bags. Pam and I were trapped on the far right side, pressed tightly against the door of the van and into each other. He leaped up and hunched right over us, way too close for comfort. We could feel his enormous power. With one fell swoop of his five inch nails, he slit our packages open. We were terrified.

I whispered to Pam, "Whatever you do, don't make eye contact." There was no escape. We kept our eyes glued to the ground and prayed that he would leave us alone. I felt like that impala. One of the men grabbed a big stick, yelling at the primate like an idiot and trying to poke at his heaving chest. Before jumping out of the van, the baboon turned on him and bared his fangs, big time. We noticed our guide was nowhere in sight. He'd disappeared up the road to hide.

We needed to rethink our adventures. Catherine had wanted to visit Durban, a seaside town with shops and tourists only a short flight from Joburg, and we'd hardly spent any time with her since landing on the Dark Continent. It was time for a quiet side trip to Durban.

15 Pandora's Box

Whenever the phone rings in the middle of the night, it's not a good sign. It must have been 3 A.M. There was a stranger on the other end of the line. I knew by the sound, the connection, and the far-away quality of the voice that this call came from overseas. It was from Thailand. The voice identified himself as someone from the Air Force. I knew what was coming next. When I confirmed my name, he told me that he was sorry to have to deliver the news . . . my eldest brother was dead. William Edgar Magner, Jr., had gotten up to shave that morning and dropped dead of a massive heart attack. He died instantly there on the bathroom floor reaching for his razor at the start of a new day. He was forty-four years young.

My brother Bill was the last of the Magner men. I am the last Magner in my clan. There is no one behind me. I wondered how many heartbeats I had left in my own breast. I returned again to Duluth to bury the last member of my family. The funeral director asked me if I wanted to see my brother, and I blurted out, "Oh gosh, no." I hadn't seen any of them to say goodbye, so why start now? I wish I had. I couldn't explain why I didn't.

I imagined my family gathering on the other side. They would have received him already, but they would be around me. Someone took a photograph of me kneeling before the granite headstone where I'd placed a single red rose. There were so many more of them over there, and just a handful of us here graveside to say farewell, to hold the flame. I never spoke for my family. I was never able to speak or say any words for them. I was struck dumb time and again. More regret. They have all come to me. They have spoken to me instead.

Some time later, two things happened that shook me considerably and served to remind me that I was truly not alone by any stretch of the imagination. I was in a studio audience for a taping of a program called *The Other Side.* James Van Praagh, who had just written a book entitled *Talking to Heaven,* was the guest that day. The author was about to take some questions from the audience. He looked at me. Someone thrust a microphone in front of me, and he asked for my question.

"Well, I lost my family in a flood and I want to know if they have a message for me," I said. James paused, looked straight into my eyes, and said, "Well, you didn't lose them all in a flood because there is another brother here."

Bill was in the house.

"He has quite a sense of humor and is telling me, 'If I can get in, anyone can.'" Everyone laughed. Then he continued: "Tell her there are really guys with white robes walking around up here." And "No, you're not finished here yet. I will be with you."

I went home and unplugged the phone. I lit a candle. I knew that my brother had been in the room with me that afternoon. There was no doubt in my mind that it was him. I felt so stupid for phrasing my question so as not to include him in the totality of my lost family. How do you get it all in with only one question?

I felt guilty for not being close to him in those final years. I felt badly for not reaching out to him, for not going over to Thailand to see him, for not calling him when I was in distress and needed my brother, my family, for not making the first move towards . . . us. I brewed a pot of chamomile tea trying to conjure his face before me. I sat there on my loveseat, and I said out loud, "I'm so sorry Bill. I love you." And then, I heard what I can only describe as a flutter directly behind me, like the sound of a large feathered wing rustling. I turned around on the sofa where I was sitting, and I saw just the tip, a sliver of ethereal movement. I blinked and it was no more.

I bent my head forward, as if in prayer, and tightly closed my eyes. My brother's voice murmured softly in my ear. "Moon, the love is never lost." What a gorgeous, perfect thing to say. Don't laugh, but that was the beginning of several conversations in which he provided me with great insight and wise council.

Another time, my neighbor Felecia, an angelic woman, came

knocking on my door one evening after I had gotten home from work. I got up and opened the door. She said, "Look, I know this is going to sound really farfetched and strange, but believe me when I tell you it happened and was as real as me standing here now. I'll be quick. Please just let me finish before you respond and then you can go back in and lie down. I know you're not well and this won't take long, but I also know I've got to tell you before I forget the details . . . here goes.

"While I was sleeping last night I had a dream within a dream. I heard someone on the stairs and woke up to see who was there. (No one ever comes to the top of our stairs unless we know them. It is very private.) So this man is climbing the steps two at a time, and I'm thinking, oh my gosh, who's here? I was a little afraid, but I was propelled onto the balcony anyway. He was standing on the landing at the top looking into my eyes, and my fear was instantly gone.

"He didn't speak to me in a normal verbal way; it was all tele-pathic, through the eyes, unspoken but very clear. He said, 'I am here to see my sister,' to which I replied, 'Well, I think she is probably sleeping.'

"I let out a little laugh at this point. I thought it was steeped in irony and, yes, obvious. He said, 'Don't worry, I won't disturb her, I just came to be with her.'

"Then he just walked through your front door."

She watched him stroll over to my couch, sit down, and put his feet up on the coffee table. Meanwhile, she said she could see me around the corner of the room, sleeping soundly on my side facing the wall, deep in another dream. I just stared, letting her finish, when she said, "Oh, and I almost forgot one thing. He had a six pack of beer under each arm."

I got gooseflesh. My brother loved beer. She turned to go and said, "He really loves you. I saw it in his eyes."

I lay down, put my head on the pillow, and pulled the covers up close around my face. I paused to listen for a moment . . . "Bill, are you there?" . . . and then I ever so delicately, reverently whispered into my darkened room, "Thank you, Bro. Thank you for coming."

We are not alone.

16 The Prognosis

Fast Forward. I was traveling again. I had two more trips planned. After an appointment with my dermatologist, I was on my way to Ireland, but I had a freckle on my face that looked "suspicious." It kept changing shape and felt a little bumpy. My doctor looked at it and said, "I don't think it's anything." Go on your trip and have a good time. "Thanks," I said, and packed my bags.

Ireland cast a spell on me. I felt an immediate affinity with the Irish. They were so kind and gracious. Being in their country reminded me of one of the first films I had seen as a child. It was *Darby O'Gill and the Little People*, and it was about leprechauns. I believed in them and spent a good part of my childhood looking for them around every tree, glade, and riverbank. In Ireland, I was a child again, cast in innocence and tinged with enchantment. The trip was good, but something was wrong. I couldn't put my finger on it. Something just didn't feel quite right. Something kept at me, pulling me away, back to LA. I was distracted and didn't know why. After six days, I was bound for home.

When I returned, there was a call on my message machine from my friend Ellen's husband. She had taken "the good medicine" and married a great guy named Greg Paul, but she was in the hospital. It was serious. She was scheduled for brain surgery to remove a tumor. I was floored. She was happy and had been healthy, strong. I drove to Cedars-Sinai Medical Center where I sat in the waiting room with Greg and her mother Billie. The news they shared was horrifying. It was radical. The tumor was large and near some important motor and nerve functions. The good news was they got it. The bad news was there was another one smack dab in the center of her brain. The second one was inoperable, but her prognosis was good.

I was at her house one day later when she pulled out a black-

and-gray MRI the size of a poster. She pointed to the tumor inside her brain. It looked like a giant acorn wedged in there. We were standing in her kitchen. On the refrigerator, I spotted a card I had sent to her long ago. It was a cartoon of a woman sneaking into a refrigerator in the dead of night that read, "Looking for love in all the wrong places." She turned around, zeroed in on the card, and then our eyes met in a moment of perfect understanding. She turned to ask me, "Mernie, do you think we'll ever get it right?"

I was still bothered by the freckle on my face that didn't appear normal to me. I phoned my doctor and made another appointment. He looked at me and repeated, "You're overreacting."

"Humor me and do a biopsy," I said.

My diagnosis was skin cancer, but not the benign, basal-cell kind that you burn off with liquid nitrogen. It was the lethal kind: melanoma. Just the word sent a shiver up my spine. My doctor was surprised. I can't imagine what made me so persistent. The doctor made a nice clean slice. It was about three inches long, over where a frown line might appear on the left side of my face. Then he stitched me up and sent me home. I figured it was a done deal. The scar would heal, and I was cancer free.

I planned a trip back to the Black Hills, and so I ran, along with my dancing partner, fear. I wanted to see my old friends and walk over the ruins of my past. A considerable piece of my heart remained in those Hills, on that ground. But again, another nudge . . . I couldn't stop this nagging feeling that something else was wrong, pulling at me to get back to LA. When I got back to my apartment, there was another message on my answering machine, this one from my doctor's office. Sure enough, the cancer was still there. They didn't get it all.

"So . . . what does this mean?" I asked. "Well, we can schedule you for more surgery next month," the doctor answered. Next month? I don't think so. How about yesterday. All I could think about was that it was growing while we were having this conversation.

I called Ellen. Over the years, she would ring me up, giving me twenty minutes to rally before she drove up the alley behind my apartment and honked her horn. Elle and I would then speed down Pacific Coast Highway and take our conversations and our therapy to the canyons of Topanga. We took marathon hikes in the Santa Monica Mountains overlooking Pacific Palisades and the Pacific Ocean. These forays lasted long into the afternoons. We lost track of time and blessedly forgot the machinations of a world that wasn't working right. Together in Nature, everything was balanced and fit. It all made sense and we did too. Here we inspired each other, regularly belly-laughed together, and paused to savor much private glee. Hate to be cliché, but we moved in the present moment, away from obligation.

I urged the doctor's office to move my appointment up. I wanted to come in the following week. "Let's just get this show on the road," I said impatiently. They finally agreed and scheduled me for the next week. The doctor's scalpel would go deep the next time.

I went to see Elle. We sat in her tranquil backyard, sipping herbal iced tea on the brick patio. We were both so young, not even half way there yet, staring at the "dis"ease in each other's faces, trying to read each other's eyes. By this time, we had no problem reading each other's thoughts. I saw her horror as she studied the long deep raw scar down the side of my face. And there I was looking behind her eyes, her lovely face, not wanting to believe she might not make it with the second tumor growing, or that I might not make it with the second surgery lurking so near, not knowing if there were more.

We reached for each other's hands, the way I'd always found comfort with friends; there in that dark theater in London with Cathy, then over darkest Africa with Pam, and now in the sunlight and the silence of this slower, more solemn afternoon with Elle. Instinctively, we reached for the human touch, the chance to feel those delicate heart muscles there in our fingertips. Words had become superfluous, too weighty, puncturing the moment. We'd both backed away from our mirrors, not wanting to confront the fear behind our own eyes.

17 Under the Rainbow

I needed a job. The money had dried up. I scoured the local trade papers in Beverly Hills. I thought I could find something in the neighborhood and decided to "follow my bliss." My passions were travel and books. Psychology was a natural draw, but I didn't believe you could heal anyone else until you healed yourself first. And I knew I was far from whole.

There was a harsh reality in front of me. I needed to pay the rent. I was living on tuna-fish sandwiches and homeopathic flower tinctures for stress—and praying for a path, direction. My ballroom days were over. I needed to live, to support myself, to keep the roof over my head. I found an ad in the *Beverly Hills Courier* for a receptionist position with medical and travel benefits. It had my name on it. The problem was they swore they didn't place it. Hmmm. Interesting. The good news was they would hire me, but I had one last hurrah in mind, and it all hinged on whether the job would wait for me while I made a quick pit stop to the land down under to see the Great Barrier Reef.

They would. Diane, the owner, gave me the once-over and said: "You can't possibly be from around here. You're too nice. If you want the job, it's yours." I liked the job description, but nice is so boring. Anyway, it was a good fit for me. It was across the street from my apartment. It would feed my need to travel, and here was an office full of other nice people. I stayed with them for six years and traveled extensively, taking full advantage of the benefits. I was so grateful.

During my years with this company, I traveled all over the world. I rafted down the white water of the Urubamba River in South America. I scaled Waynu Picchu in Peru. I skytreked over the rainforests in Costa Rica, sailed the Greek Islands, the

Mediterranean, and through the canals in the Netherlands. I visited Istanbul at the heart of the Byzantine and Ottoman empires and walked through Jerusalem and Bethlehem. I imagined the underground tunnels in Alexandria where sacred texts were hidden and contemplated the evolution of great civilizations.

I took a train through Eastern Europe to Prague, Budapest, and Vienna, hiked the Matterhorn, circled the Golden Triangle in India, and rode an elephant in Jaipur, a city awash in pink from the time when the Prince of Wales came for a royal visit in the mid-1800s. I gazed upon the Taj Mahal, the great mausoleum built by an emperor as testimony to the love of his wife. I traversed the Atlas Mountains in Morocco and the *kasbahs* of Casablanca, Marrakech, and Fez. Instead of building a career, I accumulated life experiences, collected adventures, and feasted on knowledge. Once when in a Cusco, Peru, market buying water, I caught a glimpse of O. J. Simpson racing down an LA freeway in a white Bronco on the screen of a fuzzy black-and-white television above the register.

When I decided to travel to Egypt, I called my dear friend Pam to see if she was still interested. We had talked about trying to get there when we were in Africa together. We were good traveling partners, and she felt due for a break. We decided on a Nile cruise and planned the rest of the trip around it. She flew out to LA where we boarded an outbound for Cairo. When we arrived, we sat in the lobby of our hotel with black-veiled women covered from head to toe in berkas.

The next day we headed for the Great Pyramids. It was hot. Our guide reminded us of a younger version of Omar Sharif. He turned out to be one of the most erudite and innately funny people I'd ever met. He spoke perfect English, and his knowledge of Egyptian dynasties and antiquity was spellbinding. I knew I would learn much from him and had a nagging feeling that Pam and I would discover . . . something? I thought there might be some hints here in this exotic land that I had been drawn to ever since I had read a book called *Initiation,* by Elisabeth Haich, a Hungarian woman who settled in Switzerland after World War II and taught yoga. She had what she referred to as "lucid memories" of an earlier life in ancient Egypt preparing for the priesthood.

A British woman, a friend of H. G. Wells named Joan Grant, had also penned a series of books in which she wrote of significant past lives that occurred in sacred places and historic times. She called her recollections "far memory." She wrote two set in Egypt, *Winged Pharaoh* and *Eyes of Horus*. I read them all. Of special interest to me was one entitled *Scarlet Feather* about an American Indian lifetime, and another called *So Moses Was Born*. Just fascinating stuff . . . to me anyway, and they really solidified my belief in reincarnation. When they were originally published around World War II, they were done as novels. I knew they weren't. Reincarnation went a long way in helping explain what was unexplainable to me, but I know it's not everyone's cup of tea. Pam wasn't even that interested, so I usually kept all this stuff to myself. I tended to embrace concepts that were not so mainstream, but I never shoved my beliefs onto anyone. This particular one happens to be a by-product of my death experience. It is more of a knowing than a belief.

I still hoped that being in this land of pharaohs and secrets yet-to-be-revealed would provoke some distant memory in me. We sailed down the mystical Nile River. I was filled with awe. During a hypnosis session a few years prior, I had spontaneously regressed to a significant lifetime I'd shared with Pam in Egypt. I didn't remember much of consequence except I knew we were together during an ancient time, and it was probably no accident we were together again now. Then one night when we were having dinner on the Nile, something quite unexpected happened.

That particular evening we had donned *galabias*, the traditional Egyptian dress. Pam's was a soft silken green pattern that perfectly matched her eyes. Mine was all white cotton with royal-blue piping around the neck. We even used a bit of black eye liner, smudged our eyes, and anointed ourselves in omber rose and myrrh. When I reached for my long-stemmed water goblet to take a sip, all of a sudden Pam grabbed my arm hard, trying to stop me. It was an uncharacteristic gesture, and it startled me.

She was startled, too. She immediately let go of my wrist and blinked as if to say, "I can't imagine why I just did that." Later, in the privacy of our room, Pam said, "Mernie, the strangest thing happened to me at dinner tonight." I was all ears.

"Well, when you picked up your water glass," she said, "I shifted into some other place and time. I knew there was poison in it. I just knew it. Not in the water glass you held in your hand tonight, but I was watching you from somewhere else, like seeing you on a projector." Pam had, at that moment, plugged into a time when we had previously known one another. I knew it without question.

I said in a matter-of-fact tone, "I think you saved my life in some other lifetime." She looked me in the eye and said, "Yes, I know I did." We didn't dwell on it, or discuss it ad nauseam. I'm not certain it even interested her that much, but it made her a true believer. We now both knew that our bond had been cemented centuries ago.

While we were on this trip, Pam began to seem tired but never complained. She laid down a lot with her hand resting on her abdomen. Her eyes seemed cloudy and listless. She shrugged it off. Our trip continued. We cherished this precious time together, just sitting quietly on our balcony looking out over the Nile.

Shortly after we got back to the States, Pam called to share some serious news. She had been diagnosed with ovarian cancer. Cathy convinced her to come to Cedars-Sinai Medical Center. The big medical guns out here were the best in the West, supposedly. It was an extremely intense and difficult time for Pam and her family. At times, it was touch and go. The cancer was aggressive. When she went into surgery, they found some had spread to her liver. We all worried.

While she recuperated, I came to the hospital to read to her. I read mostly stuff I had written, words that came in a sort of automatic way through me, as if in prayer. It was soothing for both of us, I think. I felt funny about sharing some of it as it was so profoundly personal, but she always asked me to bring more. Sometimes, when she was sleeping, I read to her anyway. One morning she awoke after a particularly long and stressful night. Light poured through the window and dawn washed over us.

We shared a private joke. I smiled and said to her, "Alright, my friend, now we're even." I just knew she was going to be fine. She healed.

18 Too Much to Think About

All together, I spent a decade in the travel industry—six years in Century City in a family sized "mom and pop" agency and the next four in a global corporation with offices worldwide. About my second year at work, late in 1997, when my debilitating headaches had become chronic, I was admitted to the hospital. It was about time. I was working sick, and by the end of seven years, I was exhausted from this unending, intractable pain. I had been traveling to escape. I had been traveling to lose myself. It wasn't working. The pain was escalating. I didn't know how long I could keep pretending.

I was burned out and feeling stressed out all the time. I was pulled in too many directions, and my past was still edging in on me. I was on a treadmill, moving faster and faster. I wanted off. My life depended on getting off. This script wasn't working. It was all wrong. I couldn't decipher the language of my own culture. I didn't even speak it. I'd traveled to the ends of the earth. I'd clicked my heels together. No place felt like home.

I missed my mother. I dreamed about her vividly in two distinct scenarios. In the first, she would be searching for me like an omnipotent goddess, gently calling out to me through time and the ethers. In this one, I was the prodigal daughter, moving too fast for her to catch up, staying just out of reach, always out of range, not able to make out her voice echoing farther and farther behind me. Then I turned around and became the frightened, wounded orphan in the forest. I tried desperately to find her, squinting in the twilight, losing the light until it was gone and time had run out, craving the assurance of her protective embrace, feeling it gently encircle me, while she pulled me back just in time, reminding me it was alright. These dreams made me wake up cold in my bright white room.

In the spring of 2002, I got a call from Elle. I barely said hello before I heard her say, quietly, "Mern, The cancer is growing. It doesn't look good." At that moment I knew she was dying. It was too big, too much. I told her I wished I could trade places with her, that I could take it from her, and I meant it. She had a gorgeous son and husband.

I wasn't afraid of death. I had no family to mourn my demise. Plus I was selfish: I wanted to own her death so my own pain would end. A death sentence sounded good to me. What future did I have? She had everything to live for, bursting at the seams, wanting to share it with the world. She was working on a full-length animated feature.

That summer, we saw each other less and less. She wasn't up for our old hikes anymore. Her energy was waning, she was slowing down. Her once-statuesque body was weakening and shrinking. Her reserves were depleted and her spirits low. She was beginning her descent into the land of no return. By that autumn, I was counting the days. I'd spent every Thanksgiving holiday at her home for years. I knew I would feel no abundance of gratitude this one. I assumed there would be no invitation coming, either. But she called to say, "Mern, we're expecting you for dinner." I was flabbergasted. I said, "Elle, how can you possibly think about entertaining?"

"No," she insisted. "Dinner is on. I'm counting on you to be there." I felt as if I was going to the Last Supper.

Elle reigned like a true queen until the veil dropped on December 14th. She was forty-nine years old. Her last words to me were, "Lamb . . . Mernie, turn your face towards the sun and open like the flower that you are." I wasn't fooling anyone with my shriveled up, barely beating pebble of a heart. I dreamed of her the night she died. In my dream, she was regal in a diaphanous blue gown. She smiled and whispered ever so softly in my ear, "Mern, don't lose hope." Done with earth, Elle has found her place and is gliding like Rainer Maria Rilke's swan.

Several winters pushed past me, with time moving ever onward as it is wont to do. The press of the holidays approached like clockwork with me fighting my old impulse to flee somewhere far and away. I opted instead for a picnic at Zuma Beach, north of Malibu, with Heidi, my old pal from Santa Barbara, who by this time had also moved to LA. If I was in LA without a plane ticket, I would picnic. We had done this in the past when it was overcast and absolutely deserted. We'd make ham sandwiches and potato salad and pop the cork on a bottle of champagne, making our plans for the New Year.

This Christmas Day in 2004 was more populated, but it was still a good day to be near the water, to commune with the dolphins. Heidi had another engagement and left shortly after we finished our lunch. I decided to stay put to see if I could summon my aquatic friends and breathe in some sea air. In the past, I knew that if I sat on the beach long enough, closed my eyes, concentrated, and silently called to them, they would appear, splashing and smiling, just above the waves. I plunked down into the sand and began to meditate. I waited patiently, but they didn't show. The next day the tsunami hit. I couldn't help wondering if they knew something . . . the way the elephants in Thailand did when they headed for higher ground.

I needed time to regroup, to heal the unhealed places inside of me that were begging for attention. I needed a gigantic time-out. I did what I had learned to rely upon. Beauty—in nature, music, and gentle true spirit—was the antidote for me. I tried to think of the most beautiful place on the planet. I would go there to think and tend to my soul. I told my boss, "I need to surround myself in the beauty of nature, to bathe my eyes in a glorious sunset on a private beach, and rest." Maybe God would show up. My boss understood, gave me a month off, and helped me book a flight to Bora Bora. I flew to the South Pacific where I moved into a little bungalow snug on my own beach. I waded in warm water and inhaled the ever-present aroma of exotic Tahitian orchids that permeated the air. I was on that cloud in Paradise; yet, my future hung over me like a shroud. And I wasn't well.

I returned to Los Angeles and took a short trip up the coast. I booked a room at the Four Seasons, the old Biltmore Hotel around the corner from where I'd lived in Montecito all those years ago. I put my toes in the sand on Butterfly Beach and walked in solitude, picking up broken shells, feeling broken, with the sound of my winged friends, the seagulls, overhead. I moved north farther up the coastline to El Capitan Canyon and checked into a cabin with a fireplace for a few days, surrounded by trees and the laughter of children nearby. I read, wrote, and reflected on the choices I'd made. I considered the wrong turns I'd taken, and alternately, the true grace operating in my life.

On the road back, I stopped and strolled nostalgically along the old familiar beaches I'd enjoyed when Monk had been at my side, the old haunts of those days in the 80s when I was unencumbered, loving something, which connected me to life, when I'd had no questions, only great expectations. I drove back to my apartment with a feeling of utter desolation. I'd pretended myself into a dangerous corner, a room with no doors. There was no one to call, nowhere to go, no fix. I had that old feeling that I did not belong anywhere, that my days were numbered by the math alone; all those broken hearts gone so young, too soon.

I imagined myself going back to work. Never a corporate animal, I was not fitting in this time, walking through the days, the hours, going through the motions with new superiors, too tired to learn new steps. My wings felt clipped. I just didn't know how to "do this life" anymore. I didn't seek happiness, but I sought to remember joy and to find enough peace so that my heart could heal and I could love again. I wanted the kind of love that surpasses understanding. I knew it existed because I had beheld it once, knew it existed in other realms, was how we were intended to live, but we had lost it somehow.

Periodically, I looked down to find a white feather on the ground at my feet, directly in my path. I always took this as an omen, a good sign. I maintained hope. One day, when I had just rediscovered my great, great grandfathers letters, I suddenly heard so much lovely commotion that I ran to open the door wide. There on the branch of a tree closest to me was a family of hummingbirds, so many I couldn't count them. I laughed out loud knowing that they were indeed messengers, if not members of my own family. I remembered how Sitting Bull had communicated with meadowlarks. I had the unique privilege of verifying a story I had read about him predicting his own death at the hands of his own people when he received information from the delicate bird and later it came to pass. His great grandson,

Ernie LaPointe, told me that it was true. Sitting Bull revered and communed with the animal kingdom. I now stood still and listened to the hummingbirds. A gift was being given.

Then it was time to go back to work. My month was nearing its end. I prepared myself and honed my explanation for why I needed more time. No worries. My CEO, Barry, looked into my eyes with great kindness and compassion, "Merlyn, you know we all adore you here; this is not my decision, but given the times and circumstances, we are eliminating your position." Fate had made the call for me.

I had a friend who suggested the Mayo clinic, just check in and give them my head and my body—very expensive. Or there was Brazil, a spiritual hospital. I had found an article on a healer there named John of God. He was a humble man who came upon his gifts for healing while in trance as a young boy. He passed out under a tree, and when he awoke was told that he spontaneously began to heal people. When he came to, he remembered nothing, but witnesses testified to what they had seen, and his reputation began to spread throughout his country. He always attributed his so-called miracles to God and never took money in payment. I liked the purity of this, and it sealed my decision to seek him out. Perhaps this man who only spoke Portuguese and I, only English, could find a language where words didn't matter and only the intricacies of the human spirit were understood. Maybe, just maybe, God was guiding me after all, and he had a miracle in his back pocket for me, but I would need faith. I thought my soul probably needed the healing, maybe the body would follow. The moment I picked up the page, I knew I would go.

John of God works out of a spiritual hospital he founded twenty-five years ago in Abadiânia, located in the heart of central Brazil. He is a true medium who only asks that you surrender your beliefs of what is possible and spend a minimum of two weeks there, most of which is spent in long hours of silent meditation. You may walk before him with a question about your health or even a particular condition on behalf of someone else. A translator will give you a brief interpretation on how you might be helped. While I was there, João, or John, was becoming of such renown that documentary filmmakers from all over the world, even the television show 20/20, were there along with seekers of every order. Now many books have been written about him and the Casa Dom Inácio de Loyola, and people come from every corner of the globe for serious healing of terminal illnesses or simply longing for a deeper spiritual experience. Nothing is promised or guaranteed, but nothing is taken from you either.

I found the atmosphere there to be incredibly uplifting in the midst of great suffering, a true dichotomy. I felt I was breathing rarified air in an atmosphere of innocence, along with an acute awareness of life and a sense of calm and real presence. It was grounding and enriching in a way that I am sure is unique for each one who makes the commitment to go and walk and sit and look up at the sky and feel a genuine knowing that we are all connected "here" and our lives meaningful whether we get the physical manifestation of healing, the so-called miracle, or not. It seems not to matter; only that we came and we know something we didn't know before, are changed in an ineffable way, and it is good. At least, this is what I came away with . . . and . . . heck, I had nothing to lose. The Pretender surrendered.

I took a breath and shoved off. I was in a tiny boat at sea with no compass, no oars, and no maps. The shoreline I knew was disappearing. I was being asked to trust in the wind that I loved at my back, essentially what I could not see or feel, to trust that it would take me where I needed to be.

Postcard from Home

Miami International Airport, April 3, 2005

Stay present loved one. It will be fine.
Remember to breathe. And ask for help.
We are here.
"But I feel like a total alien."
You are not alone. You are not lost.
"Tell me about it" (sarcastically).
It is but a dream, a collective dream.
The world is similar to this terminal, and your departure dates
     and
gates are all different. You are closer to home than you think.
This is what you might call "rough passage." You are in a
     corridor.
"Everything feels like a paradox."
We know the fear is strong. We know how difficult it is. If it
     were
easy, you would not have agreed to come. This feels like a
     detour, yes,
but a necessary one. You can make very swift progress here,
     so you
said, "Yes, I will come."
"It feels like superglue to me.
I feel like I have bitten off more than I can chew."
You are very ambitious, yes.
"I must have said, 'Bring it' . . . what was I thinking?"
You were thinking, "Yes, I will come again.
I will pass through the veil of forgetting and I will remember."
You would not have agreed if we had not all known it could be
     done.
"It's so hard here. I hurt all the time."
Breathe deeply.
"But I'm not feeling the love."
You have vanguards of support.

All is in order.
"Why is it so much harder than giving into the pain and
    suffering?"
There have been many cycles of earthbound suffering for the
    masses.
There is much light now and all is coming up for healing.
Be gentle with yourself and others.
As we have said, it is a bold and tender passage.
"Am I holding some doubt about my own healing?"
You answered your own question.
You are bumping up against your own resistance.

Take down your fences.
Leave the brick and mortar
To other builders of protection.
"I'm so tired I can't think straight."

The mind cannot follow where the heart leads.
Open your heart. We will heal your mind.
Just open your heart.

19 Vision Quest

Mato Grasso, Brazil, April 2005

The sky here is simply majestic. It is a map of the fingerprints of God, robust and brilliant. I look up at the clouds, fleeting kingdoms floating by, painted with pastels, hues that have no name, and sigh. It will be just a little over an hour now until I reach my final destination, a remote village situated in the deep interior of Brazil. When I arrive, time will cease to exist altogether.

We come forth from other corners of the globe to tend our battle-weary bones and mend our wayward spirits. We honor the commandment, this divine appointment to return. We converge and meet, sense the recognition, nod, and return to conversations we began centuries long ago. The gathering has begun. We're filled with hope, each of us carrying exactly what I had seen in the eyes of those hundreds of wheelchair-bound seekers in Lourdes so long, long ago when I was sixteen. We are not ordinary travelers in ordinary circumstances. We are here to contemplate and move in unison with the creatures that are effortlessly aligned with All That Is.

I watch the unfettered, eloquent dance of the audacious blue butterfly who simply beckons, "Come." I witness the tender marriage of my emotions with the elements, full and free as the rain that cries forth with the residue of my sorrow and in tandem with my joy that I have finally arrived. Here in the night sky, I stand and open like an exotic, solitary flower reaching up to the heavens to place my own fingertips on top of the constellations and connect the dots like so many specks of light mapping the way. A child emerges.

I know that our ancestors are watching, with awe and affection, as this awakening unfolds. Expectation fills the oxygen we breathe. I feel the vibration of the Fulnio Indians from the Amazon beneath my feet as they dance in celebration of the earth and sing their lullabies of praise to her. The trees respond, shaking, moving, and laughing in gratitude. I remember an ancient Thai proverb, "Life is short . . . so we must move very slowly." I will. Because I know that this is why I came—to pause, to inhale, to exhale, to be. I become still enough to hear finally the notes of my own song, my own signature, that it too may be woven into the ethers along with those who stop to listen and join in perfect harmony. In the silence, I hear a voice . . . *Merlyn, become the love that you seek.*

So, it is here we gather, for remembrance, for resurrection, to weave new dreams. Our hearts the compass, the homing devices, have called us back. The invitation has been received. The covenant is in place:

I used to worship in temples
But now I realize everything
Around me is holy
And I worship everything now.

20 The Bridge Home

On the first of the three trips I made to Brazil, which actually took place in August 2004, I met a dynamic woman who felt like a sister to me. We were thrown in together when our *pousada* was overbooked. I knew it was not an accident. Trish had been ill with cancer ten years earlier and had beat the odds. Now her "numbers" were back up, and western medicine had run out of answers for her. While I was tired and defeated, she was valiant and optimistic. If anybody had a fierce, white-hot-powerful life force, it was Trish. We became instant "old" friends and kept in close contact after our return to the States. In the ensuing nine months, we would each plan two more consecutive trips to Brazil without intentionally lining up our departure dates at the identical times.

I made the second trip back to South America in January of 2005. Trish would go on ahead to the Casa this time with the small caravan trickling in each week. I would arrive a week later with Don, who had contacted me through my travel agent when she discovered we were on the same flights. Don had brain and lung cancer, but you never would have known it by looking at him. He was a bit of a skeptic, but this remote land of possibilities for those living on the island of last chances gave much hope. The following week, Trish's sister Annette flew in from Bardstown, Kentucky.

This time, Trish wanted to tack on a sightseeing trip at the end. After some reflection and speaking with my former boss, Moshe from the small agency in Century City whom I had stayed in touch with, I suggested we travel to Iguaçu Falls, a short jaunt along the Brazilian and Argentinean border, where we would be smack dab in the middle of one of the most magnificent natural wonders of the world. I put an itinerary in place. The four of us would finish this trip to Brazil together on a high note.

At the last minute, however, I decided to extend my time and remain at the Casa, while the others went on to Iguaçu Falls without me. It was the first time I had planned a trip and then cancelled at the eleventh hour. But I couldn't leave. During my time there, I felt that I had pierced a deep truth within and needed more time to integrate it. I wanted to contemplate these feelings I had reawakened and didn't trust that I might not lose them as soon as I left. It was that powerful for me. It was difficult to say good-bye to my friends in the middle of a torrential downpour in the dead of night, to see them all off on the trip that I, the traveler, had instigated. Yet another metaphor . . . I was staying behind.

Staying in Brazil or going back to the States represented the division between the two worlds I had struggled to reconcile since the flood. My heart had opened, and I felt even more fragile if that's possible. I was both tender and fierce, convinced that my life depended on me staying put. Once again, I was clinging to my chance for survival, similar to that fateful night all those years ago when my body clung to that rooftop. It didn't have anything to do with geography. It's the place you carry with you when you don't feel afraid anymore, when you trust yourself and all that is. I needed to deepen my commitment further to insure that I would not lose this delicate and relevant passage on the tarmac of civilization.

I was standing in the middle of a bridge, close to the other side. I had essentially been in the desert wandering for thirty-three years. My heart had gone down with my family when they all left together. My body had survived, but my most vital organ, though still beating enough to keep me alive, had shriveled and closed. Love was buried in that canyon behind Jeffrey's eyes at the moment I lost him from my sight and believed that somehow I was the reason he left. Love was buried in that canyon when I saw my mother's heart break from that rooftop, and in that breath, when seeing me in the water, she must have felt helpless, that she was abandoning me and leaving me to drown and die. Love was buried in that canyon when I lost the protection of my father and I began to wander so far from home.

My heart had been buried deep and long like a fossil or a relic, the vestiges of another time. The excavation could be risky, dangerous even. It was being resurrected before me and I had to hold the space for it, to feel a measure of safety like a child taking baby steps. I had to learn to walk all over again. I had to listen carefully for God. I did not trust enough to let that happen in Los Angeles. I needed the familiar perimeters of this remote place so that the child and the woman could meet again and walk together at last.

I closed my eyes, and I picked my homesick heart up off the ground. I didn't want to drop it again. I could not afford to. I had to preserve the receptacle I had so delicately woven of the finest ether to secure it at last, find a place where it could mend and further open. I knew it would not happen overnight. It had been driven aground for so long. I must tread carefully. I treated myself reverently. I slowly became comfortable inside the womb of wonder, beauty revealed, releasing the why and choosing to embrace the mystery instead. I was in the corridor, the canal within another form of deliverance. It required patience and gestation. And my old ally fear would be there to accompany me hand in hand every step of the way.

Each time I went back to Brazil, I stayed longer and longer, and it became more difficult to leave. Was this where I belonged? Was this home? By the time I made plans to travel there for the third time, in the spring of 2005, I was running on fumes and sheer force of will. Trish would make her final sojourn there during this trip, and Don would try, but I could hear through the long-distance wires that he was too sick to come. He couldn't return, and I couldn't bring myself to leave once I got there. It was around this time that an owl appeared on the rooftop of our hotel. He was holding vigil, watching over all. He knew too much.

I ran out of money and finally returned to the States in May. I called Don. His crack humor was intact, but he sounded weak.

He collapsed in June and was gone a few weeks later. Annette flew out to say goodbye, and I sang the Beatles' song "Blackbird" to him the night before he died.

Trish flew home from Brazil and immediately planned a trip to South Dakota with Annette and her family. They wanted to pay homage to my family and visit the site of my former home. They even met Rhonda and Pam. I was deeply moved, but Trish was feeling more and more tired. We spoke the weekend she got back to Kentucky. "I think it's time to go back into the hospital Mer," she said. She was admitted that Monday. She turned fifty the following Wednesday and was gone three days later. She used to say, "This is never a battle or a struggle, only a journey." Trish was wired in a way I will always admire.

I flew to Kentucky. I sang for Trish too, the Beatles' "I Will." At last I was able to stand up and open my mouth. Within mere weeks of each other, my two companions each took a turn and a bow, and there were a pair of twin exits. It's getting crowded over there. Does it mean we didn't get our miracles, the divine intervention, the outcomes, the time, the healing we wanted when we wanted it? I believe that I am finished asking "why."

Before I left Annette's lovely home and the farm where Trish and she had grown up, we scattered Trish's ashes over the river and sojourned to another farm where a white buffalo calf had been born. According to the Lakotas, who had handed down the Sacred Pipe, the White Buffalo Calf Woman prophesized the birth of four white buffalo calves in our era, symbolizing her return to begin the mending of the Sacred Hoop to bring balance and harmony. There is more than one white calf now. The fence surrounding this newborn calf was draped with the colorful tobacco pouches of American Indians who had made the pilgrimage to bear witness. For them, it is a deeply meaningful omen. When the calves appear, it portends a time of great unification, global peace, and planetary healing. We . . . the children, on the cusp of a brave new world . . . of prophecy fulfilled.

Epilogue

Black Hills, Christmas 2007

I returned home to the Black Hills, the only home I knew grow-ing up. I couldn't wait to get to the land, to feel the sacred earth of Pahasapa beneath my feet once more. I had been away for over three decades. I had purposely stayed away, thinking it would keep the pain at bay. I almost permanently moved to Brazil, thinking that was the permanent solution for me, when one day I picked up the telephone to speak with my old friend Rhonda. I didn't even know why I was calling. She asked me point blank, "Are you coming home?" And before I could think it through, a "yes" was forming on my lips. Where did that come from?

Within no time at all, in the dead of winter, I was on the road home, braving bad roads and white-out conditions to get there. I felt an urgency to get to the land . . . the canyon where I had lost it all that night in June. Rhonda came with me while I told her something would happen. The wind would pick up or the clock would stop . . . so silly, but I needed, always was looking for . . . some sign.

I fell to my knees over the fireplace, about all that is left now besides the foundation, and began to pray. It was silent, quiet as a tomb. And then I remembered something important. Years earlier I had been back for a short visit. I had knelt down on the ground in this spot and was trying to feel something, when I dis-tinctly heard my father's voice, clear as if he were kneeling there beside me: "Darling daughter. Stand up and leave this place. Do not weep. You know I am not here. I am with you always." Powerful stuff there, Dad.

Now you can know things. I did. I got a lot of answers over the years, and I knew I had the gold standard for love, but it's not always easy when you lie down at night alone with nothing but your thoughts. I realized my biggest fear was that I would never be able to duplicate what I'd lost or settle for less, but I also realized the greatest gift of all.

I knew what love was.

Afterword

Merlyn Magner is a survivor of one of the worst natural disasters to strike the United States. The flood in Rapid City, South Dakota, in June of 1972 killed over two hundred people and is often compared to other major floods both before and after it. During the Big Thompson River flood in Colorado in 1976, for example, approximately one hundred fifty residents and visitors perished. The Arkansas River flood in Pueblo, Colorado, in 1921 killed many hundreds. And no one can be certain about the number of casualties from the Johnstown, Pennsylvania, flood east of Pittsburgh in 1889, which had the highest number of deaths from inland flooding (excluding hurricane-related disasters) in the history of our nation. As mayor of Rapid City from 1971 to 1975, I learned firsthand that floods and disasters do not always happen someplace else.

On the afternoon of June 9, 1972, the peaceful creek that flows through Rapid City, a town of about forty-five thousand people in western South Dakota, was a thing of beauty and contentment. Public fishing, high-school recreation areas, and parks, as well as residential and commercial developments filled the floodplain on both sides of Rapid Creek, which flows eastward toward the Cheyenne River. By late afternoon, airline pilots and the National Weather Service reported a concentration of heavy clouds in the area between Pactola Reservoir, west of town, and the city. Other cloud concentrations were at or near the Spring Creek drainage area to the south and the Box Elder Creek drainage area to the north. According to the National Weather Service, the densities of the clouds in these formations were identical. By 6:00 p.m., heavy rains were pouring over these creeks. The weather service was worried about one factor absent from the storm: there was no wind at any elevation to move the clouds and spread the water over the entire Black Hills.

Beginning at 7:00 P.M., the night became one of absolute terror. Merlyn Magner and hundreds of victims fought to survive and rescue family members and friends. The police department contacted me at about 6:30 to let me know the weather service had issued warnings of potentially high waters and localized flooding on Rapid Creek during the next several hours. This notification was not unusual. Storms and gully-washers are common in the Black Hills every spring and summer.

I called my best advisor, Leonard ("Swanny") Swanson, the city public works director, and we met at City Hall. Heavy rains were falling, and Swanson and I drove to Canyon Lake Park where a city worker and his family lived in a home immediately below the Canyon Lake dam. Swanny ordered the caretaker, a parks department employee, to leave the family's evening meal on the kitchen table and vacate the park immediately. It was not a gentle suggestion. It was a firm command. Every member of this family survived the flood, but not a trace of the home was ever found.

Swanny began to assemble his department heads, while I remained on the west side of town. By shortly after 7 P.M. that Friday evening, the water in Rapid Creek was roaring down the canyons between the city and Pactola Reservoir. I stopped to help a friend of mine and his crew who were pulling on a big wrench to close a shut-off valve for a major gas main that served homes above Canyon Lake. My friend put his arm around my shoulders and said, "Mayor! Somebody could get killed in this thing." The "thing" was the early moments of the 1972 Rapid City flood. It was an understatement. The crew and I watched a car float down Rapid Creek from just below the Cleghorn Springs Fish Hatchery and crash into the bridge above Canyon Lake. Minutes later, the bridge virtually imploded, and the car and debris floated into the lake.

The mayor's car had a police radio, which enabled me to monitor the radio traffic for the South Dakota Highway Patrol. What a racket came forth from that device that night! A highway patrolman was begging for help near the small town of Black Hawk, where Box Elder Creek was flooding over Highway 79. He desperately needed a boat to rescue folks who were stranded in their car in the creek. By this time, the small creek was a raging river. Box Elder Creek drains an area north and west of the city and eventually flows near Ellsworth Air Force Base. It does not run through Rapid City itself.

I radioed to Ronald Messer, the police chief, and asked him to meet me at a phone booth by the parking lot of the Canyon Lake nightclub. He arrived at the same time I did. We agreed that I should issue a warning to the biggest radio and television station in the city, asking the station engineers to forward the same warning to other media outlets. The newsman understood the urgency of the moment and recorded the warning in which I asked folks to evacuate immediately all neighborhoods near Rapid Creek and every area in the city that had a history of flooding. I closed the alert with a request for anybody who lived on the west side of town to drag a boat to the bridge over Box Elder Creek (near the old dog-racing track) and meet the distressed highway patrolman there. The radio and television station interrupted programming, issued the warning, and ran it continuously until they lost electrical power approximately thirty minutes later. It was not possible to issue a more comprehensive alert or flood warning.

During that night of terror, Merlyn and others struggled to cling to debris, to climb trees, to hang onto the chimneys of damaged homes, and prayed for strength in the face of nature's fury. Chief Messer and I, along with eight volunteers from Ellsworth Air Force Base, drove to the intersection of Second Avenue and Jackson Boulevard and tried to assist families. A four-foot wall of water was flowing down the thoroughfare, making it impossible to cross the boulevard and lead homeowners on the south side to safety. I held a battery-powered megaphone and pleaded with folks to lift their children onto the roofs of their homes. In the next few minutes, we watched these victims cling to their chimneys. It was the most hopeless moment of the night for Chief Messer and me and the courageous volunteers.

At dawn the next morning, the clouds settled to ground level, and a heavy fog covered Rapid City. It seemed like the fog of war— or the fog of death. Meteorologists later reported the absence of winds at certain elevations had caused the heavy rain clouds between Pactola Reservoir and the city to hang in the canyons and literally drip-dry during the night. Up to seventeen inches of rain fell in the canyons, and the water flowed into Rapid Creek and downstream. In town, the damaged areas along the creek were about six miles long and six blocks wide. It looked like a war zone. We knew we had heavy casualties, but we did not have any idea that the eventual number would be 238.

Under South Dakota law, civil defense is a function of county government. During the night, the county commissioners set up a central control point in the courthouse. By five in the morning, those survivors who could travel started to arrive at the courthouse and give the sheriff's office crew (the dispatcher, the jail attendant, a few deputies and volunteers, and the civil- defense office staff) the names of family members and friends who were missing. The commissioners and a few staff started accumulating the lists of missing persons. I stopped at the courthouse about seven o'clock after I was able to drive from the north side of the creek over a partially destroyed bridge on Interstate I-90 to the south side of the creek. I still remember the terror framed on the faces of the people who were reporting missing family members. They feared the absolute worst but were praying for miracles. Many broke down with worry and fear.

Words cannot describe the situation. It was heartbreaking. Later in the morning, more volunteers arrived to help write down hundreds of names. The situation became confusing, with several lists being compiled. A man from the business college across the street from the courthouse observed the developing confusion and offered to allow the civil-defense professionals to use the computers at the business college in order to combine the names from dozens of lists and print a consolidated and alphabetical listing of the missing persons. Volunteers typed the lists as the number of names increased rapidly. By noon, over eighteen hundred names had been recorded. The list grew longer through the next three days. There was order to the process, however, and the civil-defense people and the county commissioners were doing a good job. By summer's end, the list of missing would be down to twenty-five names.

Throughout the night and during the early morning hours, the police radio carried reports of shocking and terrible facts.

The police were finding dozens of bodies along Rapid Creek. I drove to the west side of town near Meadowbrook Golf Course and met Larry Lytle, the president of the Common Council. He was standing beside a police car that was towing a U-Haul trailer filled with bodies. Lytle was leading a group of volunteers and flood survivors who were retrieving bodies from the rubble in the neighborhoods near the creek, the golf course, and Meadowbrook school. I contacted the police chief to relay the idea, but he had already heard about it. All of our surviving police cars (six out of ten) went to the trailer rental office and used U-Haul trailers for the next two or three days to collect the dead. The county civil-defense office and Harry Behrens, the county coroner, managed the distribution of the bodies to the various funeral homes for the next several weeks.

The fire chief, Kenneth Johnson, and his men had worked gallantly all night to save folks from the cold, raging waters of the creek. The chief informed me over a police radio that three of his own men were missing. I had joined a crew of firemen on the east side of town near Roosevelt Park who were using ropes and ladders to pluck people from the water. Their courageous actions saved dozens of victims from waters that also contained debris, parts of houses, mobile homes, automobiles, and other materials that clogged the creek beneath the bridges. The diverted waters flooded into neighborhoods far distant from the creek. Many bridges exploded from the water pressure. The roar of the noise can only be compared to several terrible train wrecks at once or the sounds of battle that I had heard in Vietnam. By Saturday noon, the fire chief told me the names of the missing men. The body of the third fireman was not found until four or five days later, several blocks downstream from Canyon Lake near the Sioux Park Baseball Stadium.

By a fortunate coincidence, the South Dakota National Guard had assembled in Rapid City for their regular summer encampment, and the guardsmen were at their camp on the west side of the city on that Friday evening. Under the leadership of Major General Duane L. Corning, the men instantly moved into a highly professional and courageous rescue mode. They brought bulldozers, cranes, trucks, and other equipment to the banks of Rapid Creek and saved dozens and dozens of victims. I had nothing to do with the assignment or use of these men, but they were highly disciplined and well trained, and they worked absolute wonders during the night and throughout the next several weeks. Without their presence, the number of casualties would have been far greater. The price, however, was high. Several guardsmen were killed as they put their lives on the line to rescue and help perfect strangers.

During the chaos of the early morning hours on June 10th, the flood waters began to recede, and by noon, Rapid Creek had returned to normal size. County commissioners and civil-defense workers were bringing order to the courthouse. Governor Richard Kneip, his senior staff, and many state civil servants were arriving in Rapid City by convoy from Pierre. Federal officials from Denver were in Rapid City by mid-afternoon. The airport had electrical power and was operating for both private planes and commercial carriers.

The city had two hospitals at that time, and one, located near the creek on the west side of town, had lost electrical power. When I arrived there early Saturday morning, a man had driven his Winnebago motor home to the hospital and was providing emergency electrical power from his little generator. The patients were later transferred to Saint John's hospital, a larger facility that had not lost electrical power. This hospital became the main source of care for injured volunteers and flood survivors. The nurses and staff provided wonderful care, and most of the doctors in the city reported to Saint John's to manage triage and care for the victims and volunteers. I never heard one complaint about the quality of care that was provided at that overburdened hospital.

Nobody was surprised when citizens from every community in the Black Hills arrived in Rapid City with trailers and a wide variety of containers filled with potable water. The National Guard also set up points around the city to provide citizens with drinking water, using several military water trailers. In homes where water pressure was still available, folks were told to boil the water before drinking. There were no episodes of water-born disease in the flooded city or region. Within a few days, electricity and natural gas service was restored to some neighborhoods. The council authorized emergency expenditures for repairs to the water and sewer plant. On the Thursday afternoon following the flood, Don Wessel, the city water superintendent, announced that potable water was again available from the city treatment plant. With clean water available, city morale improved, restaurants reopened, and a sense of optimism prevailed. Rapid City would recover! Wessel and his technicians are the unsung heroes of the recovery.

Immediately after the flood, local Red Cross workers and national leaders of this organization arrived in Rapid City to help. George Early, the president of the Red Cross, arrived from Washington, D.C., on Sunday and supervised a system to distribute funds to the survivors. Early later told me that the Red Cross passed out over two hundred thousand dollars to disaster survivors with no strings attached.

The local commander of the Salvation Army, G. Willima Medley, and his wife were heroic during and after that terrible night. Sadly, the commander died when he drove his pickup into the raging waters to carry more people to safety. Joy Medley, despite her grief, asked me to make the city auditorium (where the Dahl Fine Arts Building is now located) available to the Salvation Army, and they would provide meals for the survivors. The city recreation director, Wes Storm, unlocked the building, and within two or three hours, an army of volunteers was serving hot meals. They managed the building throughout the summer and fed thousands. The regional Salvation Army commander from Saint Louis told me that the organization provided twenty-seven thousand meals during the first three days of recovery and over one hundred thousand during the summer.

In the immediate aftermath of the flood, our most important duties as city officials were (a) to assist those who were looking for family members and (b) to make sure that the disaster would not repeat itself. Within forty-eight hours after the start of the flood, the city council had adopted policies that were radical and farsighted. First, owners of the mobile home parks near Rapid Creek would not be permitted to repair the parks for future occupancy. Second, homeowners would not be issued building permits to repair their homes if, in the judgment of the building department, the home was over 50 percent destroyed. Third, temporary mobile homes that were provided by the Federal Emergency Management Agency (FEMA) would be set up outside the floodplain in areas where the danger of future flooding was not a factor. Fourth, the Salvation Army would be allowed to use the old city auditorium to provide meals to the survivors. Fifth, the council, using immediately available federal funds, took steps to define the geographic limits of the floodplain and the flood fringe. Sixth, the council initiated a plan to evacuate homes and businesses from the suicidal floodplain, roughly from Dark Canyon on the extreme west side of the city to the city limits on Campbell Street on the eastern boundary of the Pennington County Fairgrounds. These six items became the pillars of the recovery process.

As survivors filled motels, hotels, and private homes in the city, temporary housing became an essential need. Neighbors helped neighbors in a community atmosphere of compassion. Federally funded mobile homes were in storage at nearby Ellsworth Air Force Base until FEMA finished the bidding and construction process for eight new mobile-home parks within the city limits. The city planning commission reviewed and approved each site. By mid-July, over eight hundred families had occupied the mobile homes.

By mid-June, the Federal Department of Housing and Urban Development (HUD) had provided a planning grant of three hundred thousand dollars, which enabled the city to hire local survey crews to define the floodplain. The dollars also funded dozens of public meetings where citizens offered input on the plan to evacuate the floodplain. The formal application was submitted in early August, approved by HUD in September, and announced in Rapid City in late October by Vice-President Spiro Agnew. The plan included the relocation of over one thousand families who had lived in creek-side homes on the night of June 9th and the relocation of approximately five hundred families who had resided in apartment or rental homes in the same area. Over two hundred businesses that had been located near the stream would also be moved. A portion of the planning dollars was used to prepare a preliminary plan for the residential and commercial land within the urban floodplain that would be converted to recreational and open-space uses. These plans were popular with the citizens of the city.

Congressman James Abourezk and his staff had worked with local governments, Governor Kneip and his staff, and the federal agencies since the early hours of the disaster. A few days later, as the concept of evacuating the homes and businesses from the urban floodplain grew in popularity, Abourezk worked with his friend, Rep. Wright Patman from Texas, the chairman of the House Banking Committee, to pass legislation to enable the Small Business Administration (SBA) to provide loans to flood victims. It was a brilliant legislative maneuver. The program required the SBA to provide each family or business owner with thirty-year, 1-percent loans to purchase replacement housing and consolidate mortgages on the housing units that had been heavily damaged along Rapid Creek. Private business owners who were forced to relocate as part of the comprehensive floodplain clearance also used the program. The total federal expenditures for the four-county disaster area in western South Dakota as a result of the 1972 flood were $178 million.

The newly created Urban Renewal Agency, managed by Leonard Swanson, completed the first relocations in November of l972. Within five years following the night of the disaster, the entire program was complete. The city council dedicated all of the land as park land. Under South Dakota law, the citizens of Rapid City would need to vote to approve or reject any land sale along the banks of Rapid Creek for a residential or commercial use.

Merlyn Magner used the services of the city and FEMA and lived in a federal trailer house for several months. Her story and that of Rapid City are shining examples of how local, state, and federal programs can help flood victims and local units of government provide safe land-use patterns within an urban floodplain. Countless cities and local governments have used portions of the Rapid City plan to provide safety in flood-prone areas in highly populated urban centers and rural communities. Since the flood of 1972–and despite periods of high water along the banks of Rapid Creek–the city has not applied for one dollar of federal assistance to pay for flood damage in the urban park system in Rapid City.

The true heroes of the Rapid City flood story, however, are the victims who survived it–who refused to collapse under the strain of personal, emotional, and financial stress and moved forward to achieve both family and personal recovery. I salute the valor of disaster survivors like Merlyn Magner, who patched the strands of her life together after losing her family and demonstrated such courage and fortitude in restructuring her life.

Donald V. Barnett
Littleton, Colorado
2011

In Memoriam

The next several pages contain the names of all those who lost their lives the fateful night of June 9, 1972. May we never forget. All the people listed were known and loved by someone, and always will be. As my brother Bill so poignantly reminded me, "The love is never lost."

William Albers, William Dean Albright, Russell W. Alcott, Susan Carol Allen, James C. Atkins, Clara Atwater

Raymond Sebastian Back, James Howard Baldwin Sr., Mary Blanche Balsley, Daisy E. Barber, Henry Andrew Bauch, Valerie Jean Bauch, Roland Eugene Baumberger, Henry Beberger, Elmer Leonard Bendert, Nellie Beatty Bishop, Wilbur G. Bishop, Patricia Marlene Blomlie, Christel Blum Bostick, Matilda June Broderson, Albert Buchholz, Mary Helen Buchholz

Mary Collins Campbell, Cheryl McBride Caplinn, George Anthony Carter, Olive Pearl Chamberlain, Mary Frances Smoak Chase, Twyla Rae Chase, Joyce Christianson, Cecil LeRoy Coker, Flora Napier Allen Coker, Gertrude Coldwell, Rufus M. Coldwell, Rev. Francis John Collins, Myron Henry Corbin, Mary Bea Corner, Arla Estaline Corwin, Opal Estaline Corwin, Annette Rose Costello, Daniel Brent Crowder, Matthew Lloyd Crowder, Richard Brent Crowder, Lance Arnold Cummings, Tamara Dee Cummings

Durwin John Davidson, Agnes Detwiler, Erma Luella Dick, Lowell Henry Dieter, Patricia H. Dieter, Gwendolyn Rae Dietzel, Thomas Patrick Doherty, Joni Rodriquez Ducheneaux

Harold Peter Elliott, Ena Ellison, Gary M. Engelstad, Leilla J. Erickson, Orville J. Erickson

Robert Van Fairbank, Leon James Ferber, Noel Arthur Ferber, Sharon Lea Ferber, Margaret Fox, Raymond Fox

Alice Hazel Gall, Norvel Raymond Gall, Theophil Gall, Cathy Neal Gall, Lawrence Anthony Genovese, Martin Carl Genzler, Ruth Lonena Genzler, Jason Girton, Madeline Hazel Glover, Oliver Clarence Glover, Dale Clell Goodroad, Delores Grass, Mark Edward Greenlund

Antonie Hajek, Pearl Celeste Halff, Janice Elaine Hall, Ernest Edward Harris, Roger C. Harris, Edwin Barkley Harry, Doris M. Hausmann, Henry Hausmann, Donald E. Hausmann, Edward Everett Healey, Sheila Maria Heaton, Harry Victor Henricksen, John Fletcher Heraty, Beatrice Judd Hogan, Christopher John Hogan, Cloris M. Hollis, Wilfred Hopkins

Lois Eilene Jackson, Donald F. Johnson, Elmer Harold Johnson, Jamie Edward Johnson, William Marion Johnson, David Evan Jones, Walter Albert Juhnke

Grace Agnes Keiser, Leo Francis Kreber

Delores D. Larvie, Julia Ann Larvie, Noreen Agnes Laughlin, Anna Regina Natwick Lodnell, Edwin Francis Lodnell, Edwin H. Long

Daniel Richard MacArthur, Harry D. McPherson, Beatrice H. McPherson, Jeffrey Ralph Magner, Norma Elizabeth Magner, William Edgar Magner Sr., Leonard Magnotto, Lucy Magnotto, Jonathon Ward Masters, Stephen Ronald Masters, Timothy Wayne Masters, Otis W. Matthew, G. William Medley, Annette Mare Melby, Arlin Kilroy Mesteth, Margaret Ann Miller, Burton Harris Millett, Ida Moore, Fred Harold Morrow, Michael James Mortensen, Richard Lee Mundell

Mary Melissa Napier, Gayle Lynn Nemeti, Michael T. Neofer, Hanna New, Cora A. Newsome, Billy Wayne Nobel

Arnold James Ozuna, Ronald Joseph Ozuna, Stanley Julian Ozuna

James Wesley Patrick, Rosa Kathryn Paulsen, Marvin Eugene Pepper, Audrey Jane Petersen, Drucilla Ruth Petersen, Estel Merl Petersen, Freeman Franklin Phillips, Beth Marie Phipps, Carlo Jo Phipps, Lonelle Rae Phipps, Forrest Edgar Picht, Mardell M. Picht

Christine Ruth Quick Bear, Dennis Wayne Quilt

Ronald R. Rathman, Brenda Lea Rawlins, Frances Arlene Rawlins, Lori Jean Rawlins, Julia Ann Rawlins, Edna E. Reaves, Judy Leann Ringenberg, Tammie Jeanette Ringenberg, Neva L. Rippe, Richard Gary Rippe, Mary A. Robbins, Laura A. Robinson, Tina Robinson, Elmer Henry Rohrs, Bernnie Neil Roose, Glenn Alan Root, William H. Rough, Mable Eleanore Ruhe, Cheryl Ann Runestad, Ruthella G. Ruud

Bill Allen Sampsill, Marline Haveman Sampsill, Michael John Sampsill, Ralph Phillip Sampsill, Maxine S. Savely, Mable Alta Schullian, Edna ("Alice") Murphy Schuster, Jacob Herman Schweigman, Lucy La Roche Schweigman, Lillian E. Scriver, Randy Lee Shacklett, Claudia Lease Simpson, Eldon LeRoy Smith, Billie Claire Smith, Paula Jean Smith, Carl Eugene Smith, Gerald Wayne Smith, Jane Francis Smith, Nella Ferne Smith, Vinton Parman Smith, Elaine F. Smolnikar, Wilfred Matthew Smolniker, Louise May Sprague, Louis Star, Annette Star, Alberta Star, John J. Stroup, Geraldine K. Stuart, George Albert Sumners, Mary Louise Swanson

Roger Barner Tadlock, Henry W. Tank, Flora Ellen Taylor, William Edwin Taylor, Shannon Vale Taylor, William Allen Nelson Taylor Jr., Richard M. Tell, Jean Margorie Thomas, John C. Thomas Sr., John C. Thomas Jr., Lisa Hixson Thompson, Paul Thompson, Blake Evans Thornton, James Edward Toutges, Brand Terry Towner, Jennifer Rose Traversie, Jeremy Paul Traversie, Margaret Lamont Turner, Nellie Two Bear

Helen Jean Vanderbeek, Mark Hollister Vanderbeek, Robert H. Vanderbeek, Francis Glenn VanLeuven, Portia Faye VanLeuven, Rosemary Vogt, Anna Vucurevich

Herbert Michael Weisz, Evelyn White Bull, Herbert Loren Whiting, Phyllis Arlene Whiting, Daniel Delano Wickard, Lisa Marie Winsel, Rachel Rae Winsel, Tracy Allen Winsel

Charles J. Young

Anton B. Zieglmeier

Selected Reading and Listening

BOOKS

Black Hills Flood of June 9, 1972: A Historical Document. Rapid City, S.Dak.: Midwest Research Publishers, 1972.

Bradshaw, John. *Homecoming: Reclaiming and Championing Your Inner Child*. New York: Bantam Books, 1992.

Burston, Daniel. *The Legacy of Erich Fromm*. Cambridge, Mass.: Harvard University Press, 1991.

Cattier, Michel. *The Life and Work of Wilhelm Reich*. Trans. Ghislaine Boulanger. New York: Horizon Press, 1971.

Chopra, Deepak. *Quantum Healing: Exploring the Frontiers of Mind/ Body Medicine*. New York: Bantam Books, 1990.

Cumming, Heather, and Karen Leffler. *John of God: The Brazilian Healer Who's Touched the Lives of Millions*. New York: Atria Books, 2007.

Dalai Lama. *Becoming Enlightened*. Trans. Jeffrey Hopkins. New York: Atria Books, 2009.

———. *In My Own Words: An Introduction to My Teachings and Philosophy*. Ed. Rajiv Mehrotra. Carlsbad, Calif.: Hay House, 2008.

Frankl, Viktor Emil. *Man's Search for Meaning: An Introduction to Logotherapy*. Boston: Beacon Press, 1962.

Fromm, Erich. *The Art of Being*. New York: Continuum, 1992.

Gibran, Kahlil. *The Prophet*. New York: Knopf, 1970.

Grant, Joan. *Eyes of Horus*. London: Diploma Press, 1974.

———. *Scarlet Feather*. London: Methuen, 1946.

———. *So Moses was Born*. London: Methuen, 1952.

———. *Winged Pharoah*. London: Methuen, 1939.

Haich, Elisabeth. *Initiation*. Palo Alto, Calif.: Seed Center, 1974.

Hall, Calvin S. *A Primer of Freudian Psychology*. New York: Meridian, 1999.

Hannah, Barbara. *Jung: His Life and Work*. Wilmette, Ill.: Chiron Publications, 1997.

Hesse, Hermann. *Siddhartha*. Cutchogue, N.Y.: Buccaneer Books, 1976.

Johnson, W. J., trans. *The Bhagavad Gita*. New York: Oxford University Press, 1994.

Jung, C. G. *Jung on Death and Immortality*. Selected and introduced by Jenny Yates. Princeton, N.J.: Princeton University Press, 1999.

———. *Psychology of the Unconscious: A Study of the Transformations and Symbolisms of the Libido, a Contribution to the History of the Evolution of Thought*. Trans. Beatrice M. Hinkle. New York: Moffat, Yard & Co., 1916.

Krishnamurti, Jiddu. *Exploration into Insight*. San Francisco: Harper & Row, 1980.

———. *Life Ahead*. Wheaton, Ill.: Theosophical Publishing House, 1967.

———. *Think on These Things*. New York: Harper & Row, 1964.

Kübler-Ross, Elisabeth. *On Death and Dying*. New York: Macmillan, 1969.

LaPointe, Ernie. *Sitting Bull: His Life and Legacy*. Layton, Utah: Gibbs Smith, 2009.

Laskin, David. *The Children's Blizzard*. New York: Harper Collins, 2004.

Maslow, Abraham H. *Religions, Values, and Peak-experiences*. Columbus: Ohio State University Press, 1964.

———. *The Farther Reaches of Human Nature*. New York: Viking Press, 1971.

———. *Toward a Psychology of Being*. Princeton, N.J.: Van Nostrand, 1962.

Masters, Ronald W., and LaVonne Masters. *Some through the Flood: A Story of One Family's Loss, Survival, and Recovery from the 1972 Rapid City Flood*. Rapid City, S.Dak.: Masters Ministries, 1992.

Mendelson, Edward, ed. *Collected Poems of W. H. Auden*. New York: Vintage Books, 1991.

Miller, Jeffrey C. *The Transcendent Function: Jung's Model of Psychological Growth through Dialogue with the Unconscious*. Albany: State University of New York, 2004.

Mitchell, Stephen, trans. *The Selected Poetry of Rainer Maria Rilke*. New York: Random House, 1982.

Moody, Raymond A., Jr. *Life after Life: The Investigation of a Phenomenon—Survival of Bodily Death*. New York: Bantam Books, 1975.

Muckenhoupt, Margaret. *Sigmund Freud: Explorer of the Unconscious.* New York: Oxford University Press, 1997.

Myss, Caroline. *Anatomy of the Spirit: The Seven Stages of Power and Healing.* New York: Three Rivers Press, 1996.

Neihardt, John G. *Black Elk Speaks: Being the Life Story of a Holy Man of the Oglala Sioux.* Lincoln: University of Nebraska Press, 1979.

Ring, Kenneth. *Heading toward Omega: In Search of the Meaning of the Near-death Experience.* New York: William Morrow, 1984.

Storr, Anthony. *Freud: A Very Short Introduction.* New York: Oxford University Press, 2001.

Tatelbaum, Judy. *The Courage to Grieve.* New York: Lippincott & Crowell, 1980.

Van Praagh, James. *Talking to Heaven: A Medium's Message of Life after Death.* New York: Penguin Group, 1999.

Wiesel, Elie. *Night.* New York: Bantam Books, 1960.

Williamson, Marianne. *A Return to Love: Reflections on the Principles of a Course in Miracles.* New York: HarperCollins, 1996.

RECORDS

Armstrong, Louis. *The Complete RCA Victor Recordings.* RCA, 1997.

Beatles, The. *Abbey Road.* Apple Records, 1969

———. *The Beatles (The White Album).* Apple Records, 1968.

———. *Rubber Soul.* Capitol Records, 1965

Browne, Jackson. *The Pretender.* Asylum Records, 1976.

Bruce, Lenny. *The Carnegie Hall Concert.* Blue Note Records, 1995.

Carlin, George. *Indecent Exposure: Some of the Best of George Carlin.* Little David Records, 1978.

Collins, Judy. *In My Life.* Elektra Records, 1967.

———. *Who Knows Where the Time Goes.* Elektra Records, 1968.

Darin, Bobby. *The Best of Bobby Darin.* Capitol Records, 1966.

Doors, The. *The Doors.* Elektra/Asylum Records, 1967.

———. *Strange Days.* Elektra/Asylum Records, 1967.

Electric Prunes. *The Electric Prunes.* Reprise Records, 1967.

———. *Underground.* Reprise Records, 1967.

Garland, Judy. *Over the Rainbow.* Decca Records, 1939.

Lee, Peggy. *Let's Love.* Atlantic Records, 1974.

Mancini, Henry. *Breakfast at Tiffany's.* RCA Records, 1961.

Mitchell, Joni. *Clouds*. Reprise Records, 1969.

——. *Ladies of the Canyon*. Reprise Records, 1970.

——. *Miles of Aisles*. Asylum Records, 1974.

Pablo Cruise. *Worlds Away*. A&M Records, 1978.

Pryor, Richard. *Richard Pryor's Greatest Hits*. Warner Brothers Records, 1977.

Rydell, Bobby. *The Complete Bobby Rydell on Capitol*. Capitol Records, 2001.

Snow, Phoebe. *Phoebe Snow*. Shelter Records, 1974.

Vinton, Bobby. *20 All-Time Greatest Hits*. TeeVee Records, 2002.

Young, Neil. *Long May You Run*. Reprise Records, 1976.

——. *Harvest*. Reprise Records, 1972.